FROM HEART BREAK *to* WHOLE AGAIN

A 21 Day Devotional for Single Women

Sarah Pond

WESTBOW
PRESS®
A DIVISION OF THOMAS NELSON
& ZONDERVAN

WestBow Press books may be ordered through booksellers or by contacting:

WestBow Press
A Division of Thomas Nelson & Zondervan
1663 Liberty Drive
Bloomington, IN 47403
www.westbowpress.com
844-714-3454

Scripture quotations taken from The Holy Bible, New International Version® NIV® Copyright © 1973 1978 1984 2011 by Biblica, Inc. TM. Used by permission. All rights reserved worldwide.

ISBN: 978-1-6642-5760-3 (sc)
ISBN: 978-1-6642-5762-7 (hc)
ISBN: 978-1-6642-5761-0 (e)

Library of Congress Control Number: 2022902732

Print information available on the last page.

WestBow Press rev. date: 07/06/2022

CONTENTS

Preface vii

Day 1   Smash the Time Clock.................................... 1
Day 2   Understanding God's Love.............................. 7
Day 3   A Truly Good Father 14
Day 4   Pain 23
Day 5   The Victim.. 30
Day 6   Mind Traps... 38
Day 7   Hope... 44
Day 8   The Wilderness 51
Day 9   Worthlessness.. 58
Day 10 Codependent 66
Day 11 Understanding Attraction 72
Day 12 Finding Community..................................... 77
Day 13 Time Out.. 83
Day 14 What's The Point? 90
Day 15 Harmful Coping Mechanisms 97
Day 16 Comparison 107
Day 17 Loneliness 115
Day 18 Gift.. 120
Day 19 Matchmaker 127
Day 20 Filled With The Spirit 133
Day 21 Continuing The Fight 139

Closing Note.. 147
Acknowledgments 149
About the Author 151

PREFACE

The purpose of this transformative 21-day devotional is to begin healing your heart from past heartbreaks, create a deeper understanding of who God is, create a deeper understanding of who you are, and, most importantly, help you understand the love of God. I spent years trying to understand heartbreaks. Why they were so debilitating? Why I never seemed entirely healed from past relationships, why I could never find the "right guy," why my heart didn't ever seem safe? I don't know all of the answers, but I can tell you that along my journey, I picked up some life-changing information that, I hope, will bring the same healing to you that it brought me.

So, I am so excited that you have chosen to read this devotional. I hope and pray that it will be an ignition that lights your desire for Jesus and will allow him to heal your heart from past wounds so that you can step into the goodness He has for you. This is a 21-day devotional and was designed that way with a purpose. First and foremost, it takes 21 days to create a habit. I hope that carving out intentional time for yourself to grow each day becomes a habit. Secondly, the number 21 appears in the Bible in many circumstances relating to cleansing, salvation, reliance on God, and reset. That is what I want for you that you are reset and refreshed, ready to enter into the good promises that our God has for you.

Each day is a different topic that discusses a specific lesson God taught me throughout my single season. Each lesson contains a song that got me through the learning of that lesson. My suggestion would be to get out your Bible or Bible app (I used NIV), read the devotional, close in prayer, and then listen to the song in the car or during a time when you can be alone. Some of the passages from the Bible are included, but some I ask you to look up and read. I want you to get comfortable being in the Word. And a lot of time, it will feel like an extra step that you might be inclined to skip, but it is the most crucial step, way more important than anything I say.

You might find some topics uncomfortable or painful and feel the need to pull away. That is okay. Take all of the time you need. I only hope to encourage you to learn to be comfortable with the uncomfortable, as it will help you to grow. As you begin to push yourself in this way, you may start to unravel years of defense mechanisms that were subconsciously put in place to protect you in the short term but hurt you in the long term. It is difficult, but it is so good. If you can push through this short season of being uncomfortable, you will begin to see the fruit of your labor show in many aspects of your life.

You might not agree with all of my thoughts on the Bible and theology. In my opinion, you don't need to. I would just chew up the meat and spit out the bones, as they say. If you are offended, perhaps think about why it offends you and ask the Lord to reveal the truth you need to get from it. This may be something that He wants to change in you. I have come to hold everything loosely except Christ and Him crucified.

Anyways, let me pray for you as you start this journey: God, you know the heart of this reader, not only at this very moment but since you created them. You long for their heart, God. I can feel your longing for them in my chest. And while I might not know them personally, you have given me insight into their struggles and sadness, which overwhelms me. How you want to love them, wrap them up, and heal their wounds. God, I pray you give this reader an open mind as they turn the pages and an intense thirst for your word. I pray for endurance and peace through the difficult pages. I pray that my words are not enough and that they long to further seek your words in scripture. I pray that you make yourself **known** today. To you, be the glory, power, and honor forever and ever. Amen.

DAY 1

———∿∿∿⌒⊙⌒⊙⌒∿∿∿———

SMASH THE TIME CLOCK

♪

Song: "Fade Away - Live" by Passion
featuring Melodie Malone

I grew up in the South, where there is this ridiculous phenomenon that starts at midnight on your twenty-fifth birthday that I titled "The Rat Race to Marriage." It is this heavy societal burden put on single women, especially in the church, to find a somewhat compatible man and get married as fast as possible. Regardless of where you grew up or where you are in life, I am sure that you, in your single season, have experienced some version of this time pressure. Whether it is prompted by friends getting married, fear of fertility complications due to age, or lack of significant life achievements, it can seem like time isn't on your side. This pressure is made greater by the endless engagements, weddings, and births posted daily on social media that taunt, "You are *late* to the game! You need to start experiencing momentous life events now." And while I know that you are happy for those around you and are genuinely celebrating with them, the weight is *real*. It is something that I would bet most single women experience at some point in their life, but I am here to tell you that contrary to popular belief, time (especially in singleness) is on your side, and you can trust God with your desires.

Do not spend this *precious* time wishing it away or thinking that your life will not begin until you are married. No, this is it! Look around! This time right here is so precious. Welcome to the group I like to call kingdom singles. This kingdom is about big love, big growth, and big blessings. If you spend this season embracing this time with the Lord, you will see Him move in ways only read about in the Bible or heard of in third-world countries. You will find fulfillment that will last a lifetime and ultimately discover that you are more prepared for marriage. So, take a breath, smash the clock, and lean into what God has in store for you during this time.

Before we dive into the scripture for today, let me give you some context about the passage we are about to read. This passage was written to the ancient Israelites after being captured and put into captivity by a foreign nation called Babylon. The Israelites lost hope in God during this "exile" and thought that other gods must be stronger than Him since He allowed them to get captured. Relatable, right? How often do we turn to other avenues when we feel that God isn't working in our lives? So, this chapter is God responding to the doubts and accusations of the people of Israel. Listen to what God is saying to those of us who doubt His provision. Go ahead and get out your Bible and read Isaiah 43.

In Isaiah 43: 1-5, we get a tiny glimpse of the feelings of God toward His creation (us):

> *"You are mine"* - my heart melts when I hear this.
> *"You are protected"* - thank you, Lord!
> *"You are loved"* - by an incredible father.
> *"When you walk through fire, you will not be burned."*

Can you feel the longing of God's heart when trying to express to His creation the love that He has for us? Honestly, it must be hard to describe love with no limits to a limited human mind. And the chapter just keeps getting better. I am going to skip forward to Verses 16-21 because this stuff makes my heart sing:

> *"Forget the former things; do not dwell on the past."*
> *"See, I am doing a new thing! Now it springs up; do you not perceive it?*
> *I am making a way in the wilderness and streams in the wasteland."*

I have to admit that I don't think God is specifically talking about marriage here; he is talking about the hope for a savior, but it is more of a character statement: He is a good dad. He is passionate in his love for us; he claims us, protects us, and works in ways that we cannot see right now. Knowing those character traits of God gave me solace from the aforementioned time pressure by giving me hope for the future. Here, God says, "I am doing a new thing! Do you not perceive it? I am making a way in the wilderness and streams in the wasteland." We cannot see past this moment, but God does and is doing more extraordinary things than we could ever dream. And prior to that statement, He is describing his vast love for us. So maybe, if He loves us so profoundly, can do more than we could ask for, and is planning our future for ultimate good, don't you think that you can trust Him with your desires?

Matthew 7:7-11 says, *"Ask and it will be given to you; seek and you will find; knock and the door will be opened to you. For everyone who asks receives; the one who seeks finds; and to the one who knocks, the door will be opened. "Which of you, if your son asks for bread, will give him a stone? Or if he asks for a fish, will give him a snake? If you, then, though you are evil, know how to give good gifts to your children, how much more will your Father in heaven give good gifts to those who ask him!"*

He is moving time and space for you because He is a good father. He loves you.

My friend Ashley Smith told me this sweet story about her father that so wonderfully encompasses the extravagant love of God. Ashley did the World Race, an international mission trip where you serve in 11 countries in 11 months. After finishing the race, Ashley's flight back to the US would be connecting in New York City. She decided that it would be an opportune time to switch her flight and stay in New York for a couple of days to see the sights. She had rationed enough money to where if she could eat saltines and cucumbers for three days and stay at a cheap Air BnB, she could afford to see most of the sights that she wanted to see. Before her flight out, her father called and told her he would meet her there. She immediately knew this trip was going to be different. She knew she would be staying at a nice hotel, eating at excellent restaurants, and seeing the sights she couldn't afford to. He even told her to pick out tickets to any Broadway show she wanted to see. As soon as it dawned on her that she was now going to have her dream New York trip because her father was coming, God told her, "I am that type of father... I want you to know that when you go there, I'm there. I am taking care of you and providing for you every step of the way."

Isn't that wild?! Don't we have an incredible father? I want you to know Him on a level that you can trust that He goes before you and prepares the way.

While I might not know you, I think I know your heart. You are longing. You have scars, maybe even scars that are so deep that you can't bear the thought of being single and facing them without a partner for a moment. And I say this because I have been there. Before this single season, I was a desert. I was broken. I have been used and hurt, and I have hurt others, but welcome this stream of life that God extends to you, his child. It is refreshing and restorative. This stream makes me burst into tears (regularly) because of how it overflows, filling my soul: my once deserted, dark, and twisty soul. And this same restoration is knocking on your door right now. Will you seize the opportunity to allow God to show you his Father heart and heal you the way He has healed and continues to heal me?

The most remarkable thing about this Chapter is that Isaiah is about to predict the coming of Jesus. The light of the world, the pursuer of the hearts of the "wicked" and "disgusting." Jesus is about to straight-up wreck the world in the most beautiful way and restore the relationship between God and man. A relationship that was always meant to be centered around love. And this is the preface for that documented prediction that is the ultimate example of lavish love.

Diving Deeper:

1. Identify the different sources that tell you that you need to be in a relationship and that this time of singleness is wrong. Think about ways to stop that input so that you can take a break from it.

_____

_____

_____

_____

_____

2. What are the ways that you are currently pursuing love outside of God? Is it filling you? Ex: social media, dating, partying, etc.

_____

_____

_____

_____

_____

3. Do you doubt God like the Israelites? If so, expand on that and write it out. Lament your heart to God. He isn't afraid of your doubts.

_____

_____

_____

_____

_____

4. Is there anything God told you while reading this?

_____

_____

_____

_____

_____

PRAYER: God, you've created us whole and worthy from the day you thought of us. You looked at me and declared that I was good, especially while single. Begin the process of repurposing this time, not as a time that I use to fret over the future but as a time to understand who you truly are and what you created me to do. God, you said I am yours, I am loved, and I am protected. Open my eyes to see this and to understand it fully. As I wait for my husband, heal my heart and prepare his heart for me. I love you.

DAY 2

—∿∘⌒⊙⌒∘∿—

UNDERSTANDING GOD'S LOVE

♪

Song: To You - Maverick City Music,
Chandler Moore, Maryanne J. George

To tell you a little bit more about his love, I will let you in on a bit of a secret. The fact that you are even reading this right now means that you have heard the call. It's time. You are going to know the love of God. And once you do, you will be able to spread that love out into the world. I AM SO EXCITED FOR YOU. God is with you right now while reading this, butterflies in his stomach, waiting. He has been there all along, trying to pursue your heart, but when you turned his way today, He ran to you. His arms open wide, excited, and ready to walk you through this journey. You might think I am making assumptions about God or just trying to pull at your heartstrings, but I'm not. God pursues our hearts, and He is pursuing yours this second.

I know this because I have taken this season of my life to get to know God and His word, which is a whole book that tells about the nature and character of God. One of the authors of the Bible, David, knew God so well that God himself called David "a man after my own heart (1 Samuel 13:14)." And David wrote this about God, "Where can I go from your Spirit? Where can I flee from your presence? If I go up to the heavens, you are there; if I make my bed in the depths, you are there (Psalm 139:7-8)." If after reading that passage you began to think, maybe God is just always with David, David says this in Psalm 145:18, "*The Lord is near to **all** who call on him, to **all** who call on him in truth.*" And hey, that's what you are doing right now.

Why is He pursuing us, though? I had an incredible teacher named Andrew Shearman teach me through his poetic imagination that between the trinity, love was overflowing. The father was loving the Son, the Son loving the Spirit, and the Spirit loving the Father, creating this perfect triune love. They developed a desire to replicate that love, similar to how married couples desire to replicate their love and have children. So God created man out of that holy desire to replicate his love. That is why God calls himself a father. He loves us so much that He genuinely wanted to create us and see us grow into who He intended us to be, just like a father. But He is a perfect father. Some of us have had absent fathers, fathers who were either silent or emotionally abusive, or fathers who have passed, but God tells us He is a perfect father and promises that He will never leave us. He is with you always, even when He feels distant. When we don't think that we measure up, we tend to create this distance in our minds, but when we call on Him, He is already there.

In scripture, there is a book named after the prophet Hosea that shows the love of God differently. Usually, the love of God is framed as a father-child relationship. There is a lot of power in that view of our relationship with God. I don't want to downplay that, but many of us haven't known unconditional love from a father. The way that the book of Hosea frames God's love for us is in a covenant marriage relationship. For me, as a single woman, this brought a new level of understanding to God's love. I pray it does for you as well. It is the most insane story that brings a whole new perspective on God's all-encompassing and forgiving love and his pursuit of our hearts.

As I previously mentioned, Hosea was an Old Testament prophet sent from God to the Israelites. But instead of God giving words of prophecy to Hosea to tell the Israelites, as He did to most of the other prophets, God spoke through his life – more specifically, through his marriage. Very similar to us, the Israelites could never understand the gravity of God's love for them, and it caused them to be led astray. So, God told Hosea to marry a prostitute named Gomer. Strange way to prove a point, right? Well, you will see why in a second. Gomer and Hosea married, and she blessed him with three children. After giving birth to her third child, Gomer decided to leave Hosea. She left to pursue what we can only assume was her previous lifestyle.

I wonder what kind of lies the enemy told her that made her make this decision. Probably ones like, "Who are you fooling? You are a worthless prostitute. Stop trying to play housewife." Or maybe, "You are not good enough for your husband or your children; go back to doing what we know you are good at." See? This is how the enemy stops us from basking in the glory of God's love and blessings. He goes for our worth. No matter the reason, Hosea was heartbroken and angry. For one, God **commanded** Hosea to marry her, and this was probably his greatest fear in marrying a "harlot." And two, Hosea loved her. Gomer was HIS wife. As I write this, I can feel the heat swell up in my heart, thinking about the pain that her leaving must've caused Hosea. The pain of not being enough, the pain of losing your partner, the pain of abandonment, and the pain of a broken covenant.

Pain or not, God commanded that Hosea **get his wife and rescue her once more from that lifestyle**. Um, why? She left him. Not only did she leave him, but she left her children. Why on earth would Hosea try to find her and convince her to come back to him? Never the matter; Hosea was obedient. He found Gomer in the place of life he thought she had left behind. He paid off her debts and brought her home. He forgave her for everything and **chose** to love her despite the epic betrayal. Wow. A bold move on Hosea's part. I wonder how Gomer must've felt going from a loving husband and a family to returning to a lifestyle that, at every turn, beats you over the head with worthlessness. And how she felt when Hosea showed up to rescue her after she had betrayed him. She must've felt so wanted, saved, and most certainly unworthy of such great love. He was faithful to her. He pursued her even in the face of rejection and a broken covenant. He thought she was worthy.

The same goes for us. God pursues our hearts, and naturally (without the noise of the world), we are attracted to his love. Then the enemy appears and tells us lies of worthlessness, and we abandon that love, back to the darkness where we think we belong, back to pursuing other avenues of healing and worth. Then, He runs to our rescue even when the thing we thought would fill us breaks us. And we return with Him once more to be loved and safe. Back and forth, we run, each time breaking the heart of God. The pain He must feel, but his love for us is so deep that He will never stop. He will never stop running back to us, rescuing us from the grip of sin and shame and hoping that maybe this time, we will stay in his loving embrace forever.

Don't be held down by shame when our rescuer comes to save you. That is not what He wants. He only asks that we accept that Christ's death made us worthy, believe it, and enter back into a covenant relationship with Him. That's it. It's a pretty solid deal if you ask me. NOTHING that we do can earn our way out of that position. But in God's unconditional love for us, He sent Jesus to redeem and restore us. So at this moment, don't focus on your past or your future, instead reach up with outstretched arms to receive. Through Christ, you are worthy. Don't run away again. Just receive.

The below passage is written from God to Israel during the time of Hosea:

Hosea 14: 4-8
> *"I will heal their waywardness.*
> > *I will love them lavishly. My anger is played out.*
> *I will make a fresh start with Israel.*
> > *He'll burst into bloom like a crocus in the spring.*
> *He'll put down deep oak tree roots,*
> > *he'll become a forest of oaks!*
> *He'll become splendid—like a giant sequoia,*
> > *his fragrance like a grove of cedars!*
> *Those who live near him will be blessed by him,*
> > *be blessed and prosper like golden grain.*
> *Everyone will be talking about them,*
> > *spreading their fame as the vintage children of God.*
> *Ephraim is finished with gods that are no-gods.*
> > *From now on I'm the one who answers and satisfies him.*
> *I am like a luxuriant fruit tree.*
> > *Everything you need is to be found in me."*

We are Israel in this passage.. No matter how many times you mess up or run away, He will still love you lavishly. He wants to do incredible things through your life. You just have to let Him. You have to choose Him, and He will bless the world through you. So, as you consider the love of God, maybe for the first or thousandth time, just know that He is pursuing you. He will never stop. He created you to love you, and no matter how hard you push Him away, He will be waiting there for you, watching for the slightest turn of your head, heart pounding in anticipation for the day you choose to let Him speak tender words of love to you.

Diving Deeper:

1. How does viewing our relationship with God as a marriage covenant change your opinion of our relationship with God?

_____

_____

_____

_____

_____

2. What lies do the enemy tell you that make you run away from God's love or make you believe you aren't worthy of it?

_____

_____

_____

_____

_____

3. What are your views on God speaking to us through someone's life as He did through Hosea's? Has He spoken to you through anyone's life around you?

_____

_____

_____

_____

_____

4. Is there anything God told you specifically while reading this?

_____

_____

_____

_____

_____

PRAYER: God, you tell me that you love me, but I don't understand it. I want to know you, and I want to know the depths of your love for me. Every time I allow shame to shield myself from you, I ask that you reveal it to me and remind me of your love for me. I need your help here. Show me your heart for me. I pray that you continue your work on my heart and that you continue to prepare my husband's heart for me.

DAY 3

A TRULY GOOD FATHER

♪

Song: Goodness of God - Bethel Music

Why is there evil in the world? Why do bad things happen to good people? Why does God seem to not care about injustice? Why do I feel such deep pain? All valid questions. See, I think the root of all of these questions is the same. Is God good? As limited human beings, we have a difficult time answering this question. This question is essential, though. As a single woman, you will have to know that God is good before you can begin to trust that He has a good plan for your life. Honestly, we have to go back to the basics here, and it might be controversial or uncomfortable, but it is crucial that you know that God is good and that God has been good from the start. Let me tell you what convinced me.

God created the world so that there was no evil. He made a world without sin and sickness, without rape and murder, divorce and cheating. That was His original design. But perfect love is not forced love. Think about it, I could pick a nice guy out from a lineup and force you to marry him, and you know what, it might work out. But that isn't perfect love. That isn't the love that you have dreamed of your whole life. No, perfect love would be choosing a man and him choosing you back. It is the same way with our Father. He created us and wanted us to choose into relationship with Him, which is why He gave us a choice. On His perfect Earth, He put a tree, the tree of the knowledge of good and evil. He gave us a choice, and we chose sin. Eve chose to eat the fruit from the tree. And while, technically, the fall of humanity was not your fault, it might have been. Who knows who would've fallen prey to Satan's schemes if not Eve? Don't we fall victim to them every single day?

Go ahead and pull out your Bible and read Genesis 3.

Whether you think this story is factual or poetic, it is rich and relevant in our lives today. My favorite/ what I believe to be the most underrated part of this story is God's immediate response to Adam and Eve after eating the fruit. It is so beautifully broken and brilliant. After Adam and Eve took a bite of the fruit, they felt shame for being naked for the first time. God's reaction to Adam was not, "You disobeyed me. Now you have to die." It was, "Where are you?" If you listen to the BEMA podcast, you've probably heard this before, but it's incredible: the Hebrew word for "where" here is not interpreted correctly in English. We think, "is God joking? How does He not know where Adam is? Isn't He all-knowing?" BUT interpretation is so vital in reading scripture. If something in scripture strikes you as odd, look up the original translation and get the context. The Hebrew word for "where" here assumes that something is supposed to be there but is now missing. So God is really saying, "Adam, where are you in relationship with me? You are not where you are supposed to be. You are supposed to be walking with me."

And then the next question God asks Adam is ever so important, "Who told you that you were naked?" God is essentially saying, "you've always been naked. Why have you just now become ashamed of how I created you? What other voice are you listening to that is telling you this is not good?" See, before the eating from the tree of the knowledge of good and evil, God defined what was "good." He said animals were good, grass was good, people were good, etc. The serpent wanted Eve to determine what was good for herself, knowing that she would never know. The whole Bible is just one long story of humans trying to define what is good for themselves when God says, "I know what is good. You are inherently good. Everything that puts shame, sorrow, hurt, worthlessness, and brokenness onto you is not good. Please, daughter, listen to my voice and no one else's."

But guess what? Even though we broke the heart of our creator by choosing the knowledge of evil over living in a perfect relationship with Him, He didn't abandon us to the darkness. He gave us tools to try and make the world the place that He intended it to be while still honoring our choice. Side note, do you know how much love and respect God has to have for us to give us free will? It's more than you could ever imagine. Anyways, I know most of the world thinks Christianity is all about rules, shame, and guilt for sin, but that is not the gospel I know.

The gospel that I know is the one Jesus preached. The gospel Jesus preached while He was alive looked something like this: good news, you have a new king, and in my kingdom, we are doing things differently. In my kingdom, instead of treating the poor like outcasts, we will take care of them. Instead of stoning the adulteresses, we are going to love them. Instead of religion and rules to know our standing with God, we will talk directly to Him and have a relationship with Him. Sorry, but you can't earn your way to God now. You are in a new, upside-down kingdom.

Jesus loved everyone, especially the outcasts, and He was the harshest on the religious. He came to satisfy religion, not create another one, and He made that pretty clear. Fun fact: there were very few people groups that took care of the poor and sick before Jesus. It technically goes against our evolutionary nature to do so.

Jesus took this practice and spread it across the world. Value the outcasts above yourself, self-sacrificially love other people, emanate the love of God to everyone around you, even if they don't look or sound like you. That was the kingdom of Jesus and the good news to the world.

I believe the "rules" that everyone focuses so heavily on are guidelines so that we can begin to live in Heaven now on Earth. Think about it: a world where there is no lying, murder, crime, idolatry, jealousy, disrespect, etc., and we can rest and love our creator. Sounds like heaven, right? That world that I described is essentially the world governed by the ten commandments, and that is how God intended the Earth to be. You see, as God is love, His commandments are rooted in love for us and to protect us. As great as it would be to live our lives this way, though, it is impossible. Why? Because we are humans, and not only are we humans, but we are humans living in a fallen world with a very powerful enemy. Thank God that Jesus is victorious.

Since we had the ultimate sacrifice paid for our sins (Jesus' death on the cross), the Old Covenant is dead, and the New Covenant is alive. These rules are not a hammer over our heads for our shortcomings but are fantastic guidelines that reflect how much we need Jesus to guide us towards love. They show us that we need the help of a loving Father when we have come to the end of ourselves. Jesus even said, *"It is not the healthy who need a doctor, but the sick. I have not come to call the righteous, but sinners (Mark 2:17)."* HEAR ME WHEN I SAY THIS: Obeying the laws of God will not get you brownie points with God. You cannot earn your seat inside heaven's gates. Instead, when we have our lives wrecked by the love of God, we tend to start naturally living our lives this way. It is the fruit of our root in Jesus and an external sign that we are allowing ourselves to be guided by the Spirit of God. It is a sign of true belief. *1 John 4:19 says, "We love because he first loved us."* In order to love the best we can, we first need to be loved by God.

Have you heard the story of the Samaritan woman at the well yet? It's my favorite. Go ahead and read John 4: 1-26.

It was so simple, "Will you give me a drink?" That is all it took for the Samaritan woman to show her hand and reveal her lowly thoughts of herself, *"You are a Jew and I am a Samaritan woman. How can you ask me for a drink? (Jews did not associate with Samaritans.)."* You read the story. This was a woman who had been treated poorly by many men throughout her life. She had multiple husbands, and because of that, she carried a lot of shame. She wasn't even allowed to get water in the cool of the day with the other women. She was not trying to do this stranger, this Jew even, a favor. Then, Jesus propositioned her with an extravagant offer. *"If you knew the gift of God and who it is that asks you for a drink, you would have asked him and he would have given you living water... whoever drinks the water I give them will never thirst. Indeed, the water I give them will become in them a spring of water welling up to eternal life (John 4)."* Um.. yeah. So when she heard that proposition, she essentially said, "sign me up." Then, Jesus told her to get her husband and come back. Here is how the rest of the story plays out:

> *"I have no husband," she replied. Jesus said to her, "You are right when you say you have no husband. The fact is, you have had five husbands, and the man you now have is not your husband. What you have just said is quite true. "Sir," the woman said, "I can see that you are a prophet. Our ancestors worshiped on this mountain, but you Jews claim that the place where we must worship is in Jerusalem." "Woman," Jesus replied, "believe me, a time is coming when you will worship the Father neither on this mountain nor in Jerusalem. You Samaritans worship what you do not know; we worship what we do know, for salvation is from the Jews. Yet a time is coming and*

has now come when the true worshipers will worship the Father in the Spirit and in truth, for they are the kind of worshipers the Father seeks. God is spirit, and his worshipers must worship in the Spirit and in truth." The woman said, "I know that Messiah" (called Christ) "is coming. When he comes, he will explain everything to us." Then Jesus declared, "I, the one speaking to you—I am he." Just then his disciples returned and were surprised to find him talking with a woman. But no one asked, "What do you want?" or "Why are you talking with her?" Then, leaving her water jar, the woman went back to the town and said to the people, "Come, see a man who told me everything I ever did. Could this be the Messiah?" They came out of the town and made their way toward him (John 4:17-30)."

Just so everyone is clear, this is the first person that Jesus told that He was the Messiah. He chose this Samaritan woman who had five previous failed marriages and was living with a man who was not her husband. For additional context, the Jews hated the Samaritans. They were enemy groups – think somewhere along the lines of ISIS. Divorce was also extremely shameful in this ancient society. Being divorced once made you a social outcast but divorced five times? This woman was ostracized and shamed beyond what we can imagine. Also, just being a woman in this time was looked down on. AND THIS IS WHO JESUS CHOSE TO FIRST TELL HE WAS THE MESSIAH TO?!? Groundbreaking. Society changing. Life-altering. Transcendent of time. This is Jesus. He came to love sinners, and He proved it repeatedly.

He pointed out the shame that hung over her life: the shame deriving from the way she felt about her ethnicity, her gender, her multiple husbands, and He removed the sting from the shame because guess what? It is hard to hear the love of God when you are covered in shame. Once Jesus removed that barrier of shame for her, she finally heard His love. She heard the truth that deemed her "good" in the first place.

That is why He is good. He is good because He loves us despite our countless failures. While many people think God should just clear the world of evil, sin, death, sickness, natural disasters, etc., it isn't that easy. If He were to do that, He would have to get rid of *us* because we mess up all of the time. No, He loved us so much that He sent Jesus to die for us. God allowed His Son to die for us so that we could be, once more, in perfect relationship with Him. There will be a day that He restores the Earth to how everyone wants it to be. But in the meantime, He wants to send **us** to make it that way. We are his tools for changing the Earth.

But don't let the focus of your time in this healing process be on guilt and not living up to God's expectations. Because you know what? He knows that we can't be perfect. Instead, focus on understanding the love of God, and I am confident that your desires, interests, and actions will follow Jesus' the more you get to know how incredible He is and how much He loves you. He is good, and because He is good, you can learn to trust Him and His plan for your life during this single season and after.

Diving Deeper:

1. How does it make you feel when Jesus says that He came for the sick, not the healthy?

_____

_____

_____

_____

_____

2. Religion was what man created to know their standing with God. How does it make you feel that you're already in good standing with God and that Jesus came to get rid of religion and bring relationship instead? Do you believe that?

_____

_____

_____

_____

_____

3. Do you tend to focus on ways that you don't measure up to God's standards, or do you tend to focus on his love for you? Why do you think that is?

_____

_____

_____

_____

_____

4. Is there anything God told you specifically while reading this?

_____

_____

_____

_____

_____

PRAYER: God, we have heard many things contrary to the above, but we choose to believe in your goodness. Show us where these lies stem from and how to give the source grace and love. We are a unified body through you. Help us serve others and show them that because of your goodness and love, we can love them supernaturally. We just thank you that you are good. That you have always been good and that you are the same forever. We look to the authors of the Old Testament books, and we see that no matter what, they even proclaimed your goodness. THANK YOU for your love.

DAY 4

———⟊ঙ⟊ঙ⟊ঙ⟊———

PAIN

♪

Song: Defender (LIVE) - UPPERROOM

*"In the world you will have troubles. But take heart;
I have overcome the world." John 16:33.*

After what seemed to be a long, rocky 3 to 4 months, my 2-year long relationship ended. The night that it ended, we had a huge fight. I called an Uber, grabbed everything I could carry, and left his apartment. I don't remember it too well, but what I do remember is waking up the very next day thinking, "Is this real? Did I really just end my relationship?" With uncertainty, a slight hangover, and the fear of the pain of loneliness clanging like the absolute loudest gong in my head, I ran to God. I ran as fast as I could. So much so that I felt late. I spent days crying, reading scripture, books, devotionals, anything I could get my hands on that related to God. And He softened the blow, held my hand, and reassured me that my decision was the right decision for both of us. My first reassurance was that I knew I needed a partner that would point me back to Jesus, which He was incredible but did not.

Second, I saw physical signs from God that He was there and ready to pull me deeper. Everything I was reading, seeing and listening to confirmed the life-altering path that I so haphazardly chose.

Then, more pain. I saw a picture of my ex, not even three weeks later, with another girl. It was probably just a friend, and I mean, I broke up with him, so it was very okay that He was in a picture with another girl, but my brain was not a healthy place. So yeah, it hurt. I remember that I started lamenting to God, "Why God?! What did I do to deserve this?" And this is what I love about God: He didn't say, "Let's review, shall we?" Trust me that could've gone on for years. No, because that is not the character of our God. In Psalm 34:18, we read, *"The Lord is close to the brokenhearted."* And He indeed was. He wrapped me up in His arms and comforted me. He did such an excellent job that by the end of a five-hour crying session spent with the Lord, He changed my heart. He allowed me to forgive my ex by showing me his hurt, and God allowed me to understand the goodness that was really in my heart: that I sincerely do want what is best for him. This conclusion did not come out of my own strength and stability. You don't know me, but wow, coming to that conclusion is nothing shy of supernatural.

I just want to explain what you might not know. God can actually heal your pain and change your heart. It may take days, weeks, months, or even years but run to Him. He will reveal Himself to you as the God of comfort. *2* Corinthians 1: 3-4 says, *"Praise be to the God and Father of our Lord Jesus Christ, the Father of compassion and the God of all comfort, who comforts us in all our troubles, so that we can comfort those in any trouble with the comfort we ourselves receive from God."* So your pain is not in vain. He will use you to comfort others with it, but first, He will comfort you. So, pray, lament, find scriptures or devotionals, and listen. You will experience pain in this season, but don't fear that pain because He has overcome the world. He will rescue you, redeem you, and set you on the right path: a path that is even better than you could ever imagine.

Also, you should know that our God is a God of compassion. He grieves when you experience deep pain. The best example of this is found in the shortest verse in the Bible, "Jesus wept." (John 11:35) Why? That's another great story:

So, He left Judea to spread the good news of the kingdom, but on His journey, a messenger sent word to Him that Lazarus, His dear friend, was very ill. Jesus did not change His course and stayed two more days preaching when He received word Lazarus had passed. He decided to head back to see Mary and Martha (Lazarus' sisters). When He arrived, the town was mourning. *"When Mary reached the place where Jesus was and saw Him, she fell at His feet and said, 'Lord, if you had been here, my brother would not have died.' When Jesus saw her weeping and the Jews who had come along with her also weeping, He was **deeply moved in spirit and troubled**. 'Where have you laid him?' He asked. 'Come and see, Lord,' they replied. **Jesus wept.**" (John 11:32-25)*

Isn't that beautiful? His heart was broken by the sadness that the people felt. It broke His heart. He wept. He even knew that He was about to raise Lazarus from the dead. He knew the end result: Lazarus would live! But He still cried because the people that He loved were grieving. He loves us dearly and weeps at the sin and brokenness in the world. He weeps, even though He knows the end outcome: He will be victorious in the end. And He will redeem you and lift you up when others hurt you. Don't let that be the focus during this time but know that your pain is not going unnoticed. Your God will prevail.

Also, I'm just going to place this right here:

> *Romans 12: 17-21*
> *"Do not repay anyone evil for evil. Be careful to do what is right in the eyes of everyone. If it is possible, as far as it depends on you, live at peace with everyone. Do not take revenge, my dear friends, but*

leave room for God's wrath, for it is written: "It is mine to avenge; I will repay," says the Lord. On the contrary: "If your enemy is hungry, feed him; if he is thirsty, give him something to drink. In doing this, you will heap burning coals on his head." Do not be overcome by evil, but overcome evil with good."

God says to love your enemies and pray for those who persecute you, but God is for you. His wrath is not against flesh and blood, but He does tell you the best form of "revenge." Instead of seeking to hurt others because you yourself are hurt, be kind, and it will actually **"heap burning coals on his head."** This sounds intense, but it is a reference to a time when people who were poor would put a container that could safely carry coals on their head and walk around asking for burning coals to take home to keep their fire burning. So by "heaping burning coals on their head" it is actually helping them. What a metaphor right? The people who hurt us are lacking and by being kind we are giving out of our surplus to help those who can only take.

Let's instead look at some verses that you can hold on to when you experience emotional distress (the Psalms are such a great place for this):

Psalm 34: 17-22
"The righteous cry out, and the Lord hears them; he delivers them from all their troubles. The Lord is close to the brokenhearted and saves those who are crushed in spirit. The righteous person may have many troubles, but the Lord delivers him from them all; he protects all his bones, not one of them will be broken. Evil will slay the wicked; the foes of the righteous will be condemned. The Lord will rescue his servants; no one who takes refuge in him will be condemned."

[Side bar: if you are thinking, "I am not righteous. He isn't talking about me." He is. He has made us righteous through Jesus.]

Psalm 147: 1-6 Praise the Lord. How good it is to sing praises to our God, how pleasant and fitting to praise him! The Lord builds up Jerusalem; he gathers the exiles of Israel. He heals the brokenhearted and binds up their wounds. He determines the number of the stars and calls them each by name. Great is our Lord and mighty in power; his understanding has no limit. The Lord sustains the humble but casts the wicked to the ground.

Psalm 94: 16-19 Who will rise up for me against the wicked? Who will take a stand for me against evildoers? Unless the Lord had given me help, I would soon have dwelt in the silence of death. When I said, "My foot is slipping," your unfailing love, Lord, supported me. When anxiety was great within me, your consolation brought me joy.

Psalm 31 (all of it)

Psalm 18 (all of it)

Psalms 23 "The LORD is my shepherd, I shall not be in want. He makes me lie down in green pastures, he leads me beside quiet waters, he restores my soul. He guides me in paths of righteousness for his name's sake. Even though I walk through the valley of the shadow of death, I will fear no evil, for you are with me; your rod and your staff, they comfort me. You prepare a table before me in the presence of my enemies. You anoint my head with oil, my cup overflows. Surely goodness and love will follow me all of the days of my life, and I will dwell in the house of the LORD forever."

AMEN. Wow, that is beautiful stuff. I especially love Psalm 23. I always visualize God taking my hand and guiding me through all of those settings. He does that, though. He takes our hands and guides us through this life. This life that sometimes feels lonely and uncertain. That tests us and beats us down. David says that when we face these trials, we are not alone. God is a place of solace. He is taking our hands and leading us through. In the presence of our enemies, we are not alone. We are never alone because His love will follow us all of the days of our life.

Something that a lot of other studies won't tell you is a road map to healing. Why? Because there isn't one. There is no right or wrong way to heal, and your journey will look different than other peoples'. The Holy Spirit transcends processes. God will take you down His path of healing personally designed for you because He loves you and knows your heart and what YOU need individually. While I'm not going to give you a roadmap, I will provide you with some resources later on to explore.

Diving Deeper:

1. When you get upset or start to feel pain, what is your immediate reaction? Do you dive into the pain, or do you cope immediately?

   _____

   _____

   _____

   _____

   _____

2. Is there anyone else in your life experiencing a similar pain? Take some time to pray for them and an opportunity to comfort them or serve them.

   _____

_____

_____

_____

_____

3. Write out one or multiple of the above verses and meditate on what it means to you.

_____

_____

_____

_____

4. Is there anything God told you specifically while reading this?

_____

_____

_____

_____

PRAYER: Wow. God, the pain in this world, the pain in this reader. We long for the day when you will restore the Earth, but we are thankful to be here. You are Jehovah Rapha, the Lord that heals. Show them your comfort. Give them your peace and reveal yourself to them as the God of Comfort that you have said that you are.

DAY 5

———⌘———

THE VICTIM

♪

Song: Graves Into Gardens (Live) -
Elevation Worship, Brandon Lake

W e've all been hurt, right? If not, I doubt you would be reading this devotional. I just wanted to address the obvious because what we do with that pain is pretty definitive. For many of us, the natural reaction is to internalize the hurt, react in hurt to others, and then victimize ourselves: blaming others for what happens to us and for our actions. And if you, like me, experience this, it's okay, but there is more for us. Sometimes we tell ourselves lies like, "No one will stay around long enough to love me." And "It's not worth meeting nice guys because nice guys aren't attracted to me." Or, "No one cares about me." We think we have very little control over our relationships, careers, outcomes, etc., but that's just not true. That is exactly what the enemy wants us to believe. He wants us to think that we don't have control and are powerless. Psychologists term this as an external locus of control: a person who attributes their successes and failures to fate or external factors as opposed to an internal locus of control: someone who believes they are in control of their life).

How can an external locus of control be negative? Having an external locus of control is usually correlated with higher rates of depression and anxiety. People feel out of control, helpless, and unable to make a change in their own lives. Often, it is learned from a parent or stems from physical or mental abuse. No matter the case, we are not victims. When others hurt us or life doesn't go as planned, we know that we are more than conquerors because God is with us. He controls the outcomes of our lives. He enables us with the tools and strength to fight back.

It is fascinating; there is this misperception that all Christians have an external locus of control, that God has planned all of their life, so they don't have to participate in making tough decisions. And honestly, I get that. God says that He is sovereign, and He is in control of our lives, and we believe Him as we should. But we don't just sit down and let life happen to us, taking punches left and right and letting life beat us up. No, He wouldn't be able to use us if we just stopped moving. We have to MOVE. Like I previously stated, He has equipped us with tools, given us the Spirit of God, and made us able.

> *Romans 8:37-39*
> *"No, in all these things we are more than conquerors through him who loved us. For I am convinced that neither death nor life, neither angels nor demons, neither the present nor the future, nor any powers, neither height nor depth, nor anything else in all creation, will be able to separate us from the love of God that is in Christ Jesus our Lord."*

What does that look like? How do we conquer instead of victimize? We do this by shifting our external locus of control to an internal locus, understanding that God is ultimately in control. That is confusing, right? We live in accordance with the way Jesus lived. We use the tools of the Kingdom: truth (the word of God), peace, salvation, faith, the Spirit, and righteousness. We trust that by living within His commands, we are on His path, which is the absolute best path for us. You have to remember that God is looking at our lives from a bird's eye view. We can only see time as it passes. We have to trust his bird's eye view over our own.

I think many people stay paralyzed, waiting for God to move all of the pieces together so their life looks like what **they** want it to be. I even fall prey to this fallacy myself. In my past career, I worked for a company that had a Christ-following leader. When I got the job, I knew God placed me there, but after working there for a couple of months, I realized the company's culture was toxic. It truthfully was a chaotic, self-esteem-breaking mess. Since I thought God placed me there, I felt that I needed to take up my cross (if you will) and endure the toxic environment to be a light to balance the darkness. One awful day at work, I walked into the bathroom, got down on my knees, and cried out, "God, please rescue me." When I got home that night, I started moving and applying for jobs. I had absolute peace about applying for jobs like I never had before.

I applied, and within a month, I got a job offer. I actually got two job offers at the same company, which doesn't happen a lot at this company. HR had to get involved and balance the salary offers to make it a fair choice. LET ME TELL YOU WHAT… that was God. My interviewing skills are not excellent, and my experience level was minimal, but all things are possible with God. I prayed for a rescue, and that was it. But I went TWO AND A HALF years not moving and falling victim to a job I knew was toxic. I just complained, victimized myself, and tried to get sympathy so that people could understand my pain. I believe that God could still use me and that I learned a lifetime of lessons in those two years because what the enemy uses to harm, God uses for good. But, since I left that company, I have found so much more peace. It is pretty impossible to find peace in a toxic environment.

I didn't tell you that story to tell you that God will always bless you when you take action, pray, and live within his commands. That isn't what we are signing up for at all. In fact, most of my life spent with God; I received answers to prayers that I didn't like. One out of 10,000 was when I asked for healing when my father got sick. I prayed and prayed for him to get better, but he did not. He passed six months after his diagnosis of brain cancer. That was the very beginning of a lot of trauma in my life. God doesn't promise us that He will only bless us in the ways we think are best, but He asks us to trust Him and continue moving. He has a way of taking the ashes of a horrible situation and using the good that remains from them to bring life to others.

We know that we have to take action, as I previously said, but the best part about it is that instead of all of the pressure falling on us if we fail, we have peace from knowing that if we fail, God is sovereign. And let me repeat this for emphasis, what the enemy intends to harm us with, God uses for good! God always wins.

I got that saying from a verse in Genesis, which comes from the story of the Israelite Joseph. He is the best example of a victor in God and someone who had every excuse to be a victim but did not succumb to it. Some background on Joseph: he had at least ten brothers, and they hated him because he was his father's favorite. His father favored him so much that his brothers plotted to kill Joseph. But Instead of killing him, they sold him into slavery. He became the slave of a man named Potipher in Egypt and rose in the ranks of Potipher's household. So much so that Potipher entrusted him to run his whole household, which was a tremendous job. One day, Potipher's wife tried to seduce Joseph, and when he did not give in, Potipher's wife accused him of rape. Joseph was then sent to prison for a long time. In prison, Joseph interpreted the dreams of a few men and eventually was called upon by Pharaoh to interpret his dreams. When Joseph interpreted them correctly, Pharaoh made him one of the highest-ranking officials in Egypt. One day, his brothers came to Egypt to get food because there was a famine in the land. And because of Joseph's leadership, Egypt was able to store up an ample food supply to sustain them during the famine. They came to Joseph, and HE was the one to decide whether or not to give them food so that they could live (Genesis 37-50).

> *Genesis 50: 18- 21 " His brothers then came and threw themselves down before him. 'We are your slaves,' they said. But Joseph said to them, 'Don't be afraid. Am I in the place of God? You intended to harm me, but God intended it for good to accomplish what is now being done, the saving of many lives. So then, don't be afraid. I will provide for you and your children.' And he reassured them and spoke kindly to them."*

To summarize, Joseph was attacked and thrown into slavery, not because he did anything to wrong his brothers other than being a little arrogant, but because he was his dad's favorite. Then, he worked hard as a slave and rose up in his master's household only to be falsely accused of rape (for doing the right thing) and then thrown into prison.

Do you think he was tempted to victimize himself and his circumstances? Yeah, I bet so. He was probably thinking, "God, this is so unfair. I have lived well according to your commands and have worked hard. WHAT ARE YOU DOING TO ME?" But instead, he kept moving and kept his faith in God. He once again rose up because he had God on his side. He became one of the highest-ranking officials in Egypt because God equipped him with the skills to do so.

In relationships, if you constantly feel like you aren't good enough for people to stay around for, too broken to be loved, or even that you have to stay in a bad relationship because you won't find anyone else: know that is a lie. The enemy wants you to sit there and be paralyzed. But here's the thing – you have the power of the Holy Spirit in you. God has equipped you with the tools to be more than conquerors. If you want to find a Godly man, you have to discover your true identity in Christ. Spend time with God and let Him tell you who you are— whether that is in therapy, reading self-help books, reading scriptures about your identity, or spending time outdoors waiting on the voice of the Lord. If you want to find a Godly man, surround yourself with God-fearing, respectful friends. Find a community of true believers who act like Jesus. If you are confused about what Jesus acted like, just look at how He reacted to people groups: the poor, the widows, the religious, the adulteress. This will give you an idea of the kind of man you want in your life.

Some of my friends, including myself, at times, have expressed the desire for one type of man, but then we find ourselves with another - the kind that hurts us. This predicament has a lot to do with attraction, which I will discuss later. If you are currently here, I want to tell you that the enemy has you right where he wants you, afraid and paralyzed. Pray and ask Jesus to give you the strength to choose to leave, and God will be there to walk you through the pain. You can either wait until the pain of inaction becomes more significant than the fear of action, or you can step out in faith. When you step out in faith, He will honor that by pulling you closer. God will love you no matter what you choose, and He can pivot around our choices even if they don't align with His. Aligning with His plans is to your benefit, though. If you think the man you are with isn't God's best, there are probably reasons like habits, temperaments, etc., that if you look down the line, will worsen or lead to more extreme behavior. By choosing to align your will with God's, you choose less future pain for yourself.

If you are on the other side of this circumstance, you have to choose your next partner like you are going into a battle because that is what you are doing. A God-fearing marriage is powerful, and the enemy hates it. He hates unity, so ask God to reveal the tools that your husband needs to fight this battle alongside you. The less stress, distrust, and misalignment in your relationship, the more you can focus on pouring out love on other people.

At the same time, work on your relationship with God and try to become the person you're looking for is looking for (as famous pastor Andy Stanley would say). And that might mean investing some time and money in counseling or seeking out a mentor in the church. There is such a stigma around counseling that it's scary, or worse, "only for insane people." That is the enemy trying to hold us down because he knows the good that comes from counseling.

You are not a victim. Your past, your feelings, and your experiences are valid. But God has already redeemed you. You haven't lost. The world is not against you when God is for you. You are brand new, so what are you going to do now? Let life happen to you? God has given you the power of the Spirit. IT LIVES WITHIN YOU. All you have to do is lean closer to God because, in your weakness, He is strong.

Diving Deeper:

1. Identify places in your life that feel out of your control.

   _____

   _____

   _____

   _____

   _____

2. What are small manageable goals you can set to impact those out-of-control places in your life?

   _____

   _____

   _____

   _____

   _____

3. Are you willing to trust in God's overall plan if it doesn't turn out in the way that you deem good? If not, it is okay, but God wants you to talk to Him about it.

_____

_____

_____

_____

_____

4. Is there anything God told you specifically while reading this?

_____

_____

_____

_____

_____

PRAYER: God, thank you for giving us your Spirit. Help us see that we are not victims of circumstance, but we can transcend circumstance with your help. Show us the next steps to take and prevent us from feeling overwhelmed. We love you so much, and we are choosing to believe that we are more than conquerors.

DAY 6

MIND TRAPS

♪

Song: Prince of Peace - Hillsong UNITED

"Self-discipline begins with the mastery of your thoughts. If you don't control what you think, you can't control what you do." - Napolean Hill.

Before we get started, I should note that Jennie Allen's book 'Get Out of Your Head' inspired a good portion of this section. If you enjoy this section, you might want to give it a read..

I am not going to pretend to know who Napolean Hill is, but I think it is obvious where I am going with this. I'm going to begin by telling you about the toxic thoughts that were swirling through my mind when I first became single again and jumped back into my relationship with the Lord:

"What if God wants me to remain single for the rest of my life? I'm not okay with that."

"If God doesn't give me my husband by age 30, I
will just lower my standards."
"Does God want me to give up the love of my life
for Him because he is not a Christian?"

These are the kinds of mind traps that the enemy uses to distract us from tackling the task at hand: healing so we can bring the kingdom and spread God's love to those who need it. Once these thoughts enter our minds, we abandon the quest for healing and redemption and seek immediate comfort. Or, in the case of my past self, seek a boyfriend. The following sentence is important: your thought life impacts your whole life. It is important to know that you are not your thoughts, and you can learn to take them captive, but ultimate healing will come from God. As daunting and exhausting as it probably sounds, you can do this because you aren't alone. The key to doing so, as the incredible author Jennie Allen said, "is knowing that you have a choice." You have a choice to think about the thoughts that overwhelm your mind. You have a choice to go down those dark and twisty rabbit holes of shame, guilt, and not being good enough. I understand that some people struggle with mental illnesses and chemical imbalances. I have walked through that battle myself, but you have a choice whether or not to meditate on them.

I have mentioned the "enemy" a couple of times now, assuming that you know who I am referring to. I think it is essential to call it out. The Bible asks us to believe that there is a spiritual realm, and in this spiritual realm, there are dark beings: satan and demons. They are working against us and constantly oppose God and His goodness. They do not want us to combat negative thoughts, because as I previously mentioned, our thought life controls everything. We have to learn to fight back.

Even if you don't believe in demons or Satan, classical physics and psychology tell us that something in the world, and our minds, pulls towards disorder and destruction. I think the fact that entropy exists is a decent case for this, but also psychologist Sigmund Freud said our mind is divided into three parts: bad, deciding, and good or the Id, ego, and superego. On a non-spiritual level, what is great about Christianity is learning that the bad part or the id is not who you are. It is an external force that is not a part of your being. Learning to not identify with that "bad" helps that part of you quiet and helps you learn to love yourself and see yourself the way God sees you.

The best advice I ever received was from a friend who was getting Christian counseling. Her counselor taught her to develop a secondary voice in her head to combat the loud inner critic or negative voice within. Since my inner critic was so vociferous, I decided to practice that as well. My secondary voice started out soft and was something I had to practice intentionally. Still, it became more automatic as I practiced mindfulness, studied scripture, and prayed for God to enter into my thoughts. The key here is studying scripture. In order for your voice to speak truth into the enemy's lies, it has to *know* the truth. God cannot bring His words to your mind when you need to hear them if you do not ever learn them. His Word holds power; power over shame, guilt, lust, lies, and more. They aren't just empty words of encouragement. They are God's words of truth, and we need them to fight back.

When I start to think one of those negative thoughts and my heart begins to sink, my secondary voice kicks in to nullify the whole train of thought. It looks a little something like this:

> **Me:** What if God never wants me to get married?

> **Voice:** God loves you. God values his relationship with you. He designed you and gave you that desire for marriage. (Psalm 139:13-16). He will do immeasurably more (Ephesians 3:20).

> **Me:** If God doesn't give me my husband by age 30, I will probably just settle.

Voice: God has a perfect plan for your life that you cannot even begin to comprehend. Each day he is working for my good. He is all-knowing, and I am limited in what I can see. (Romans 8:28)

Me: Does God want me to sacrifice the love of my life for Him?

Voice: You think you have felt love, but it was a limited human love. What God brings is more than that. He quenches your longing for love with streams of life everlasting and a love so deep that you will not thirst any longer (John 4:13).

I am sure it sounds a little exhausting to combat negative thoughts continually, but that voice will begin to automate. It takes a minute to develop, though. It will get stronger the more scripture you read and the more time you spend in solitude with Jesus. Before you know it, the negative voices will begin to quiet, and there will be room to hear the voice of the Holy Spirit speaking clear and loving thoughts, giving direction, and reminding you of the promises of God.

Paul says in *2 Corinthians 10:5, "We take captive every thought to make it obedient to Christ."* Our brain is moldable, and we can form new neural pathways by taking our thoughts captive and choosing to think thoughts that align with Christ. Over time those new neural pathways will become the default, and the old ones will go dormant.

If that sounds too difficult, instead, stop what you are doing and just start reading scripture or listening to a Christian podcast. Don't allow yourself to sit on your worries and focus on the things out of your control. Singleness isn't a terminal illness. It is a part of life and an important one at that. Focus on Jesus. Keep Him as your true north. Accept that today you will be single and lean into what God wants you to do with that. I can tell you one thing: I would have never started to write without this time of singleness. So, ask how God wants to use you today and focus your thoughts there.

Let's open to Philippians 4: 8-9

> *"Finally, brothers and sisters, whatever is true, whatever is noble, whatever is right, whatever is pure, whatever is lovely, whatever is admirable—if anything is excellent or praiseworthy—think about such things. Whatever you have learned or received or heard from me, or seen in me—put it into practice. And the God of peace will be with you."*

Learning to take your thoughts captive is just another step in this process. God wants us to release our control, know that He has our future in His hands, and then step out in faith and think about lovely, admirable, noble, true things. I am not saying that you should avoid all feelings. Beautiful things happen when you work through the pain, but choosing to trade in ruminating on damaging lies or thoughts for meditating on God's truth and his love will bring you life.

Diving Deeper:

1. Where do your thoughts spend the majority of their time outside of work? Write out a list of places where your mind vacations for most of the day. Are there any feelings that are associated with it? Write them out.

   _____

   _____

   _____

   _____

   _____

2. Write out Philippians 4: 8-9 on a sticky note and put it on your bathroom mirror. Read it every time you brush your teeth this week.

_____

_____

_____

_____

_____

3. Is there anything God told you specifically while reading this?

_____

_____

_____

_____

_____

PRAYER: God, we want mental freedom. We want to think your thoughts of love, peace, and life. Be the road sign in our minds to remind us that we choose what path our thoughts go down. Help us take captive every thought and lay it at the feet of Jesus. We are so eternally grateful that you have given us these tools to set us free. You are truly the prince of peace.

DAY 7

HOPE

♪

Song: Promises - Maverick City Music,
Joe L Barnes, and Naomi Raine

Wow, this right here is so important, so listen up. My best friend sent me this incredible sermon on hope preached by Adam Young. Honestly, I don't know him, but he is so kingdom. In his sermon, he discusses what the Lord says regarding growing a relationship with Him. *"And now these three remain: faith, hope, and love. But the greatest of these is love." 1 Corinthians 13:13.* I am sure you have heard this before, but what I have always heard people preach about this verse is the last sentence, "The greatest of these is love." While that is true, **all three are necessary**. Then Adam gives this definition of hope that changed my life.

> **Hope:** *groaning inwardly while waiting expectantly but wrestling with God in the interim about why it hasn't happened yet.*

Do you feel that on a spiritual level or what? Dude, being single while the whole world seems to be walking down the aisle is one massive serving of 'inward groaning.' It is that longing for a husband unfulfilled. The desire to get married and be loved in that way, unmet. So great! We are a third of the way there, right? The next part is the key: **waiting expectantly**.

<u>WARNING:</u> this is unadvised by the majority of the population. Everyone lives in this constant state of protection. We don't want to get our 'hopes up' for any reason but primarily for fear of the pain of losing something. Something that what? Something we never had in the first place? I think the enemy is tricky here. He says, "if you hope in the Lord, He will disappoint you. You can't trust Him. There is no way that He will fulfill this desire for you. Don't hope, don't trust. Take control." But God asks us to trust Him and wait expectantly.

Here is the thing: a lot of pastors will make sure you know that God doesn't promise that He will give you a husband. And they are right – nowhere in the Bible does it say, "God is going to give you a husband 1000%." To me, those were probably the most discouraging words a pastor could say. They killed my hope because I figured that I would be one of the ones God would want to stay single, even though I longed for a husband more than anything. It made me so sad. And once again, to believe that God will fulfill all of our desires on this earth is inaccurate, but God does say that He is a provider. He tells us not to worry because He will do more than we can even think of. So while I can't tell you that God has promised 100,000%, you will get married, I do believe there is a reason God created marriage and a reason He put that desire in you. That desire is biblical. It aligns with his will. I think God is a safe place to put your hope in and a safe God to trust. The walk of a Jesus follower is not going to be the easiest, but I do believe God gives good gifts to those who follow Him and seek His heart. So don't be discouraged. He is a haven for your hope.

This last part in the definition of "hope" that Adam gives us just seems plain wrong: "wrestling with God about why He hasn't given it to us yet." WOAH. But wait, isn't God all-knowing? Isn't His timing perfect? Didn't you just say to trust Him? Doesn't He know the desires of my heart? In Isaiah 49:23, God promises the people of Israel, *"those who hope in me will not be disappointed."*

Adam says something very profound about wrestling with God. While he acknowledges that no, not all of our longings will be fulfilled in this world, he says something so simple and true, "We don't know which ones will be!" He claims that most of us don't want to wrestle with God because we don't want to engage with Him, hold Him to his promises, and fight with Him about giving us our desires. I honestly had not been doing this prior because I thought it was disrespectful, and I didn't know it was allowed. But here is the kicker. He says not to surrender our desires to God until we have had a long, tough, 12-round boxing match with our Maker about it.

Wrestling with God changed the game for me. I was trying to surrender daily the longing for a husband. I would pray, "God, please give me a husband, but only if it is your will." And every time that desire appeared in my mind, I would shut it down by surrendering it to God. The issue with that is, I never really duked it out with Him, and my daily surrendering wasn't working. So I took a stab at battling with Him.

My true inspiration for my battle was Jacob from the Old Testament. To me, Jacob used to be a controversial character. From the time he was born, Jacob was fighting for the family blessing, and he would do anything to get it. His name even meant deceiver. He came out of the womb grabbing the heel of his twin brother, Esau, trying to fight his way out first to become the bekhor, meaning the firstborn heir. His birth foreshadowed the day when Jacob would deceive his blind father and steal the family blessing from Esau. Jacob received the family blessing, but even that wasn't enough for him. Every chance he had to take what he wanted, he did. Take a look at this story below:

Genesis 32: 24-30:

> *"So Jacob was left alone, and a man wrestled with him till daybreak. When the man saw that he could not overpower him, he touched the socket of Jacob's hip so that his hip was wrenched as he wrestled with the man. Then the man said, "Let me go, for it is daybreak." But Jacob replied, "I will not let you go unless you bless me." The man asked him, "What is your name?" Jacob," he answered. Then the man said, "Your name will no longer be Jacob, but Israel,[a] because you have struggled with God and with humans and have overcome." Jacob said, "Please tell me your name." But he replied, "Why do you ask my name?" Then he blessed him there. So Jacob called the place Peniel, saying, "It is because I saw God face to face, and yet my life was spared."*

Weird story, right? Some people may think that Jacob actually wrestled with God who came to earth, some people may think it is just a story, but either way, the point is that God wants us to wrestle with Him. Jacob wrestled until God blessed him. And guess what?! GOD DID BLESS HIM. Even though he was branded from birth as a deceiver. God blessed him and gave him a new name that would be great among the nations: Israel. The name of his people. That's big. God chose to make a nation out of Jacob even though he lied and stole the blessing from his brother Esau, which Esau traded him for a bowl of soup. See, God would rather partner with a fighter who had hutzpah like Jacob than an apathetic man like Esau. So, put on your gloves and start the match. Engage with God. Cry out to Him and ask for your hopes and desires. You are allowed and even encouraged to. Once you have lamented and put up the best fight you can, then you can start surrendering. Then you can honestly mean what you say when you tell Him, "if it is your will."

I am not saying that you should be putting your hope in your plans but instead put your hope in God and His character. I had this bad habit of hoping in timelines and saying, "I think 2019 will be the year I meet my husband." That is optimistic, not hopeful. We are not mind-readers. We will get exhausted if we put our hope in timelines. Instead, hope in Jesus. God gave you the desire for marriage and hope in the fact that He says not to worry about the future and that there is a reason why. GOD LOVES MARRIAGE. It might not be right now, but He will provide. If you wait on a good man of God, you will see that you did not misplace your hope.

After the fight, surrender to God. **You will begin to notice that your will will align with His. You will see that you can trust Him because every time you are obedient, He will be there guiding you, and you WILL see His good works.** It is UNREAL. When you let go of your timelines and your plan for your life, God will show you the goodness of His plan. And IT IS NOT SMALL. IT IS ABUNDANT. God wants to use you and will use you if you let Him, and when it unfolds, blessings will pour out. The kingdom of God is about abundance. The kingdom of earth is about scarcity and fear. In God's kingdom, there is no room for that. So when you think, "there are no more good, kind, beautiful men of God out there." That is a scarcity mindset. We are in the kingdom of ABUNDANCE. In Matthew 6:33, Jesus says, "But seek first his kingdom and his righteousness, and all these things will be given to you as well." So don't be afraid to hope and to step into what God is calling you to now. The enemy wants you to be frightened. He wants you to think, "If I move to that city where I think God is calling me, I am going to delay me meeting my husband." He wants you to think, "If I break up with my boyfriend because God is calling me out of this relationship, I will regret it. I will never find someone else." But God is saying, "Trust me. I am a good Father. I love you. I have what's best for you. Come deeper, my beloved, and I will satisfy you."

So, hope in the Lord. He will do immeasurably more.

Diving Deeper:

1. Are you afraid to hope in God? Lament to God about your longing below. Really flesh it out here. Begin the fight.

    _____

    _____

    _____

    _____

    _____

2. Can you think of ways God might be wanting to use you right now?

    _____

    _____

    _____

    _____

    _____

3. Are you stuck in a scarcity mindset? If so, are there practical ways you can think of to meet new people to begin to see the number of good men out there?

    _____

    _____

    _____

    _____

    _____

4. Is there anything God told you specifically while reading this?

_____

_____

_____

_____

_____

PRAYER: You are our fortress. You're a safe place to put our hopes and our dreams. We know that not all of our desires will be filled on this Earth, but we also know that you have put desires on our hearts. We choose to put our hope in you. We choose to believe that your character is good. Help us even know what to pray for as we begin to tell you what our heart desires. We love you, and we trust in you and your story.

DAY 8

THE WILDERNESS

♪

Song: Isaiah's Song - Maverick City Music

itling this section 'Wilderness' is risky. In the Old Testament, the Israelites entered the wilderness after being rescued from slavery by Moses. The wilderness is often synonymous with wandering, testing, and a lack of faith in the Bible. It was not the best of times for the Israelites, but it was intended to be. I have a quick history lesson for you taken from the Bema podcast episode 22. The Old Testament/Old Covenant between Israel and God was modeled after an ancient Jewish wedding ceremony. There were ten significant parts to a traditional ancient Jewish wedding ceremony.

1) The Betrothal period: This is the time where the Groom and his father would go to the Bride's family to make arrangements for a marriage covenant to be formed.

We see this in the covenant made between God and Abraham when God tells him to leave his father's house (Genesis 12:1). Men during this time never move away from their father's houses. As you will see in a minute, the men build additions onto their father's home and continue under their provision. When God tells Abraham to leave his father's house, He essentially asks Abraham to leave his community, his family's religion, safety, etc., to trust God and begin a new way of doing things with Him. This is the beginning of his covenantal marriage relationship with God.

2) Groom leaves to prepare the house: The Groom would then return home to his father's house and begin to build an additional section onto his father's house where he and his wife would live after the wedding ceremony. The building process could take anywhere from 1 to 2 years. During that time, the Bride's family would begin preparations for the wedding. The expectation was that whenever the Groom arrived at his future Bride's house that her family was prepared and ready to throw the wedding feast on that very day. Even if he came back at 3 am, they would need to be prepared.

In the Old Testament, God goes silent for 400 years while the Israelites' are enslaved by Egypt. He is preparing for the bride (Israel) to enter into a covenant with Him.

3) Arrival of the Groom: After preparing the room for his future family, the Groom would return to his Bride and begin the celebrations.

We see this play out in the exodus story (when Moses saves Israelites from Egyptian slavery). God returned to take His bride, Israel, with Him.

4) The Bride is consecrated: Once the groom returns, the bride would be consecrated or prepped for her wedding day.

God tells Moses to 'consecrate Israel' or prepare them for the covenant (Exodus 19:10).

4) Shofar is sounded: Then, the family would sound the Shofar or a ram's horn.

In the wilderness, the ram's horn was sounded so the Israelites would know that the Lord was going to come down on Mount Sinai in the sight of all the people. (Exodus 19:16)

5) Choppah: The next significant piece of the ceremony was the chuppah, which was essentially the altar the bride and groom stood under that represented the presence of God.

At Mt. Sinai, there was a thick cloud covering surrounding representing the presence of God (Exodus 19:16)

6) Ketubah: The groom would then present the Ketubah (terms of their covenant) to the bride, and she would either accept or deny them.

The ten commandments represented the terms of Israel's covenant with God (Exodus 20).

7) Consummation: Next, the bride and groom would consummate the marriage.

The Tabernacle was the place where the presence of the Lord would be with the Israelites. A space where they could be with Him in close relationship (Exodus 26).

8) Exchange of gifts: After the oddly public announcement of the consummation of the marriage, the groom would exchange his gift with the bride's family.

This gift to the Israelites is "The law," which you can find in Leviticus. It is hard to imagine in our 21st-century western culture that any law is a gift, but through the lens of an ancient Israelite, it was a gift to establish rules of engagement with God (Leviticus).

9) Honeymoon year: Once the ceremony was finally over, the two would leave to go live in the new addition to the groom's father's house, where they would spend a honeymoon year. During the honeymoon year, they would not work at all but get to know each other deeper.

The wilderness season was supposed to be a honeymoon period where the Israelites would get to know their God more deeply and have a close personal relationship with Him. Let's see how the whole story played out:

God told Moses to lead the Israelites out of slavery, redeem His people, and lead them to the promised land. So Moses went to Egypt and fought with Pharaoh time and time again to get the Israelites freed. But of course, Pharaoh didn't want to give up his slaves, so God sent horrible plagues to Egypt. Finally, after the last plague killed Pharaoh's firstborn son, he agreed to let the Israelites free to stop the plagues that God sent to Egypt. Almost instantaneously, Pharaoh changed his mind. He ran after the Israelites, an entire army in force. And the Israelites witnessed a powerful miracle. They were trapped between the sea and the Egyptian army, and God used the wind to PART THE SEA so that the Israelites could escape. WHAT?! That is beyond (Google realistic images of what it probably looked like. Scary, right?). So you would think that the Israelites knew that they could trust God, right? Wrong. Moses led them into the wilderness to escape and what should have taken around 11 days to travel from Egypt to the promised land took 40 years because they strayed from their path and their hearts strayed from God.

You see, The Israelites approached the promised land in the first year. They even sent spies into the promised land to check it out. The spies confirmed all of the goodness that the Lord spoke of in the land, but there was one issue: the people that currently inhabited the land were huge in number and physical size. The Israelites were terrified and angry when they heard this. They didn't believe that God could help them take the land. Think about that. They just experienced God bringing them out of slavery by sending plagues on the Egyptians (miracle) and parting the sea (miracle), but they thought He drew the line at clearing a city? Plus, the whole point of this journey was to get to their destination. Why would God take them this far not to get the Israelites to the promised land? God allowed the Israelites to wander to refine their faith and refocus their attention. The Israelites wandered so long that they **wanted to turn around and go back to being slaves**! Can you believe that? Why on earth would these people want to leave their mission to the promised land to go back to being slaves?

Do you see where I am going with this? WE DO THAT ALL OF THE TIME. We begin our single season confident and assured that God has better plans for us. But when God doesn't send us our husband immediately, we lose sight and run right back to the comfort of either an ex or jump immediately into a relationship with someone we KNOW is not God's best.

I think the key here is focus. The Israelites were focused on God when they were enslaved. They prayed day after day, they wept and mourned, and God **saw** them. He saw their tears, and He rescued them. Once He saved them, they abandoned Him and turned to other gods almost immediately. They broke their marriage covenant with God. This wilderness period was supposed to be a honeymoon period where they would fall in love with their creator, and He would return that love to them and provide for them. Their focus was on getting out and getting the promises of a flourishing land, and when God didn't deliver in the way they wanted, they were done with Him. God was offering them more than just the promised land. God was offering them **total fulfillment** by a relationship with Him. It might be hard to think about that during this time. Complete fulfillment just by being in relationship with God? It is possible. The closer you get to God and the more you can receive His love, the more the world around you quiets. It is the most beautiful, serene, and loving experience that a human can have. All of this to say… marriage sounds incredible, just like the land of milk and honey, but are you sure it will fill that inner longing? I'd say looking at divorce stats, it isn't all that it is cracked up to be. God is offering you so much more.

Once again, I'm not saying that God is holding out on you until you do things for Him like donate, volunteer, read your bible, etc. That is faith by works. You do not have to do anything to earn God's love. Also, you will not be able to control the amount of time you are in this single season by how fast you heal. I feel the need to clarify that because that is what I thought once upon a time. As soon as I broke up with my ex, I wasted no time and tried to compound the healing process to move on and find a husband. Two years later, I am probably getting to the crux of my issues. You can either take this season and utilize it by growing your relationship with Jesus in your honeymoon time or wander trying to find love and worth through unfulfilling avenues. I promise you that you will find a fuller life if you choose the first of the two options.

Don't lose sight of the goal, don't turn around and go back to slavery when the promised land is in your future. When I say the promised land, I am not referring to marriage. The promised land is a relationship with God and lasting fulfillment that marriage just doesn't meet. So, focus on Him during this wilderness. Make it a real honeymoon between you and God, where you get to know Him and hear His voice.

Diving Deeper:

1. What do you think God could be wanting you to learn during this period?

    _____

    _____

    _____

    _____

    _____

2. What other "gods" do you turn to when God won't deliver? Ex: social media, partying, etc.

    _____

    _____

    _____

    _____

    _____

3. Is there anything God told you specifically while reading this?

    _____

    _____

_____

_____

_____

PRAYER: We need you, God. We want this time with you to be the honeymoon it was meant to be. We want to focus on you and know you. Give us the discernment to know how to make the most of this time. As we grow with you, take us to further depths of your love for us.

DAY 9

─────wwↄↄↄↄↄↄↄ─────

WORTHLESSNESS

♪

Song: As You Find Me - LIVE
Hillsong UNITED

Worthless: having no real value or use (Oxford Languages). Wow... that's a harsh word. It's one that I don't think of too often. I will be honest here; I have never really considered myself worthless or of no use. See, I enjoy the person that God has created me to be. And when I think about my life, I feel like I have brought value into the world. But even though I know logically that I am not worthless, I could never put a name to the pain I would feel when triggered by breakups, rejection, or jealousy. It is normal to feel pain in those circumstances, but this pain was too deep. It wasn't "normal." It would just sit like a burning coal in my chest ardent until I paid full attention to it. And once I did, I could never piece together why it was so sharp and intense. After seeking Christian counseling, I learned that I couldn't see that my emotions and actions were a symptom of a deeper wound: **worthlessness**, wrapped in **denial**, and topped with a beautiful bow of **pride**.

Let's establish the ground rules of worthlessness, shall we? The first is that it is sneaky, like a parasite. When you're in emotional pain, you often won't notice it's caused by worthlessness, but it is there, and it is extracting joy from your life. The second is that it affects all of your decisions, actions, reactions, and emotions (so important). It can be set off by something as simple as a basic rejection, like someone you know not waving to you at the grocery store. Something so small can bring on such a giant reaction. The final, and I would say most important, is that it completely blocks you from understanding the love of God.

Since we are already talking about singleness, let's use a personal example of an ex moving on. When I broke up with my ex, and he moved, I was so upset, and my pride was genuinely hurt that I had such a strong reaction to something so trivial. I have been through some dark times, and honestly, I was disappointed in myself that my heart ached so deeply when I saw my ex with another girl. But, I could never pinpoint my exact feelings about it. I expected not to be bothered by it at all. I chose not to be with him. So, why was I so sad? What was lying underneath that was causing all of this pain? Worthlessness. You might not make that association right away. That is okay! I didn't, either. Let me try to explain further the way it works.

Worthlessness is always associated with an experience. When you experience rejection, bullying, abuse, slander, etc., the enemy shoots you with little arrows labeled, "You are useless. You are not beautiful. You aren't smart enough. Just admit it; you are of no value to this world." The messages of worthlessness **carry the pain**, not the experience. If you think back to a moment of rejection, it isn't necessarily the words that someone said or didn't say that was the most painful. No, it was the why. "Why does he think that I am not good enough? What is wrong with me? Am I not educated enough? Am I not pretty enough?" The worthlessness is the source of that deep and indescribable pain that we feel, but why is it so powerful?

It's like learning about rip tides. You can read about them for months in textbooks: about their strength, power, and deception, but have you ever been in one? When you're caught and can't get out, you **know** the strength, power, and deception of a riptide. The experience carries fear and emotion. So much so that you could even develop a phobia of the ocean or a distaste for going to the beach. The experience holds significantly more weight than just reading about it. That is how this works. You have experienced difficult events that ingrained this deep wound of worthlessness in you. I can sit here for hours and tell you that you are a loved daughter of God with infinite value, but you will not understand it because your experience of worthlessness trumps my voice of encouragement.

That is the same with the love of God. You know that logically God loves you. You may have been told this your whole life, but your experience of worthlessness is deeper than a friend's voice telling you, "Hey, Jesus loves you!" When you can learn to break down your walls by giving the worthlessness that is deep within you to your Savior, you experience the freedom and love of Jesus.

Here is the best news, your Dad in heaven loves you so much, and He knew that the enemy would use worthlessness to attempt to steal you from His love. And it breaks Him. He weeps for us when we experience pain. So, He did something about it. Something so extravagant that shook the earth. He sent His Son, Jesus. He sent Him to love the unloved, heal the broken, cast out demons in His name, show His power, satisfy religion, change the relationship between God and man, and restore worth to the worthless. He did it in perfect love. Although Jesus lived a perfect life and didn't deserve the wicked death cast upon Him, He willingly walked into it. Jesus went to the cross, and on the cross, He hung there in agonizing pain because you're worth it. If everyone on Earth was saved but you, He would do it all again just for you because you are so worth it. He hung there essentially asking you to **give Him your worthlessness, your failures, and your mistakes, to give Him your "not good enoughs,"** and in return, He would make you whole again. You have a fresh new start. Everything that you have done in your life has been wiped clean. The blood of Jesus was the physical sign of this. So go ahead, look up at the cross, hand Jesus the worthlessness that the world has put on you and be clean. All Jesus asks for in return is for you to believe in his unconditional love and to follow Him. What a beautiful love it is.

> ***Psalm 139:14*** *"For you created my inmost being; you knit me together in my mother's womb. I praise you because I am fearfully and wonderfully made; your works are wonderful, I know that full well. My frame was not hidden from you when I was made in the secret place, when I was woven together in the depths of the earth. Your eyes saw my unformed body; all the days ordained for me were written in your book before one of them came to be."*

> ***Luke 12:7*** *"Are not five sparrows sold for two pennies? Yet not one of them is forgotten by God. Indeed, the very hairs of your head are all numbered. Don't be afraid; you are worth more than many sparrows."*

> ***Ephesians 2: 4-9*** *"But God, being rich in mercy, because of the great love with which he loved us, even when we were dead in our trespasses, made us alive together with Christ—by grace you have been saved—and raised us up with him and seated us with him in the heavenly places in Christ Jesus, so that in the coming ages he might show the immeasurable riches of his grace in kindness toward us in Christ Jesus. For by grace you have been saved through faith. And this is not your own doing; it is the gift of God, not a result of works, so that no one may boast. For we are his workmanship, created in Christ Jesus for good works, which God prepared beforehand, that we should walk in them."*

I feel like these words have lost some of their power because we've heard them so many times. But, He created us, intricately, with love! And because of that love, He covers us in His grace and mercy. Because of the blood of Jesus, we are free. If we repent and believe, every sin is covered, past and future. He dubbed us worthy of this incredible and beautiful sacrifice. While Jesus was in the garden of Gesthimite, sweating blood from his pores, asking God if there was any other way, He thought of you. He thought of what people in the world would do to hurt you. He thought of all of the moments that you would cry and scream out to Him in pain and because He loved you so much, He chose to go through with it. He went to the cross. An innocent life ended to begin an epic kingdom of worthy and loved followers.

THE MEDITATION:
My therapist walked me through the following meditation that wrecked me, and I would like to give you the option to read it and meditate on it.

"Imagine you are living in the time of the Old Testament. It is the night before Passover. You go to your sheep pen and choose the most spotless and perfect lamb you have. You set him aside in a separate pen and go inside to go to sleep. You wake up before the sun and go outside. You tie up your sheep to a rope and begin your walk to Jerusalem. The city is two hours' walking distance, which is great because it gives you time to think. You start to think about all of the sins you have committed since last year's Passover. Maybe you yelled at your spouse. Perhaps you had a lustful thought about someone outside of your marriage covenant. Perhaps you didn't pay all of your taxes to the government. Take a minute to think about the sins that you committed.

Off in the distance, you see Jerusalem. You are approaching fast. You look down to see your spotless lamb and make your way into the city. At the temple, you get in line, ready for the sacrifice. You get to the altar, and the priest helps you lay down your lamb. You think one last time about your sin, and the dagger enters the lamb. It is done. The priest fills the cup with blood, and you know that all of the sins you committed since the last atonement are forgiven because of that blood. You are clean. Every sin has been wiped away, and you are brand new.

Fast forward a couple of months, and you hear the townspeople talking about a man called John the Baptist. He is preaching down at the Jordan River, baptizing people and telling them, "Repent for the Kingdom of heaven has come near." So, you decide to see what all of the fuss is about. While you are at the river, you see a man approach. This man was unlike any other you had seen before this moment. He approached John asking to be baptized, but John, stunned, said, "I need to be baptized by you, and do you come to me?" John baptizes him, and you see a dove-like Spirit descend from the heavens, and you hear a voice that says, "This is my Son, whom I love; with him, I am well pleased." So you begin to follow him.

You leave everything behind and follow him along his journey. You see him heal the blind, heal the paralyzed. You see him give worth to a woman who had six husbands. You see him love the wicked and bring judgment to the church leaders. He ate with the people who everyone hated and was disgusted by, and He loved them. You even saw him raise a man from the dead.

Fast forward to Passover three years later, and you are sitting at the table and eating with him. He took the bread from the table and passed it around and said, "*This is my body given for you*" He then held up his wine and said, "*This cup is the new covenant in my blood, which is poured out for you.*" Confused, you do as He says. Then, you follow him out to the garden of Gethsemane, and you see him in distress. He is sweating blood. And you see off in the distance a large crowd of people coming in your direction. There he is… Judas. Judas approaches Jesus and kisses him, and Jesus willingly walks with them.

You then see him on trial. The crowd accuses him of all of these charges that you have never heard of? They were false; the crowd didn't understand. This man was innocent. This man was holy. You are relieved when you hear that Pilate didn't sentence him to death. But the crowd is angry. They won't rest until he is dead. When Pilate finally gives in, you see them beat him. They whip him, 39 lashes. They then get out a cat of nine tails and beat him further. A few soldiers put a crown of thorns on his head and beat it in. They force him to carry a cross with his limp body to the place where He will be put to death. They start with his hands and nail them in. Then his feet. Next, they add a sign mocking him, "King of the Jews." You look up to him … and you see his blood. And He asks you to give him all of your shame, your worthlessness, your pain, your past, your sins, your life, and you are clean.

That blood was the blood of the covenant. You may now receive His love, worth, life, and spirit. He has redeemed you, and you are new. Everything in your past is atoned for. You are free from the chains that bind you. You are clean."

Let's take a moment and pray. God, we cannot even begin to imagine your love. It doesn't seem fair that Jesus, a perfect man, your son, would have to die for us. Who are we to deserve this? But God, I pray that tonight we don't focus on our worthlessness but instead that you deemed us worthy, worthy enough for Christ to die for us. Thank you for His life and death. We receive your love tonight. We rebuke any shame or thoughts holding us back from you. Help us receive this gift. Thank you, Jesus. We love you forever and ever. Amen.

Diving Deeper:

1. Are there specific moments in your life that Satan used to steal your worth? Write them below.
   a. I want you to notice the pain of worthlessness separated from the actual memory.

b. Pray over these experiences. Picture Jesus being there, weeping with you. Ask him where He was?

_____

_____

_____

_____

_____

_____

_____

_____

_____

_____

_____

_____

_____

_____

_____

2. Is there anything God told you specifically while reading this?

_____

_____

_____

_____

DAY 10

---✿---

CODEPENDENT

♪

Song: Refiner - Maverick City Music

Since we just discussed worthlessness, let's talk about one of the sneakiest ways it manifests in relationships: codependency. I have forever been battling codependency. What is that, you ask? It is essentially anxiety over someone else's problems and life choices. The official definition is a behavioral condition in a relationship where one person enables another person's addiction, poor mental health, immaturity, irresponsibility, or under-achievement. Among the core characteristics of codependency is an excessive reliance on other people for approval and a sense of identity (Wikipedia)." If you are in or ever have been in what some might deem an 'unhealthy relationship,' there is a considerable chance that you act in a way that is dependent, codependent, or both. Being aware is the first step in changing "unhealthy" relationship patterns so that future relationships will thrive.

I'm going to give you an analogy that my therapist gave me that he paraphrased from Rabbi Edwin Friedman to illustrate codependency further:

Pretend you are on a bridge, and someone you don't know comes up to you. You see that they have a rope tied to their waist, and they ask you to hold it. You agree, grab it, and they jump off the bridge without a second thought. You are almost thrown over the side of the bridge from sheer force. You scream down in anger and ask, "what are you trying to do?" The stranger answers, "don't let go. You are responsible for my life." You try to pull the stranger up, but they are too heavy, and they refuse to help, claiming, "you just holding on will be enough." Your arms begin to weaken, and you devise a plan. You tell them, "If you loop the rope around yourself, you can climb up loop by loop." But they once more refuse and say, "My life is in your hands. Do not let go.". You are now faced with a choice... you can either let go of the rope and save yourself or hold on until you both fall over. After much back and forth, you warn them that you will let them go if they do not agree to come back up. The stranger says, "you wouldn't be so selfish." Then, you decide to give back the responsibility of the stranger's life to themself by letting go. In that example, the stranger is the dependent, and you are the codependent (Rabbi Edwin Friedman).

I was hit with immediate anger when I was first told this story because I knew that my therapist meant that I was codependent and that I either needed to accept my fate or let go of the rope. But I love helping others, and I do not mind sacrificing myself to do so... isn't that what Jesus did? Aren't we supposed to love others at the expense of ourselves? I mean, He sacrificed himself for us. My therapist pointed out that if you look closer at the story, you can see that the stranger who jumped off the bridge didn't want help. They just wanted the codependent to hold them up. Every time the codependent thought of a way to help, the stranger refused. Finally, the codependent removed themselves from the situation because while they tried and tried to save the other person, they could not, but they could save themselves.

Our inner critic has a way of making us think that we should stay in an unhealthy situation to help someone who is struggling.

Sometimes to the degree that it takes over our lives. After my ex and I broke up, I decided to keep the line of communication open in case he needed me (which I convinced myself was good for both of us). Because of this, we essentially extended the emotional relationship instead of ending it like we agreed to. I thought I was helping him by giving him advice and telling him how awesome he was, but I was hurting him. And honestly, I was hurting myself too. I hurt him by extending that relationship and probably giving false hope of us getting back together. I tried to fix his pain and tell him how he should live his life, again taking over as I did in the relationship. I was hurting myself by feeling a false sense of security and (here it is) worth because he still "needed me" and prolonging the feelings of love and relationship. That is the deep motivation for codependency. Either you are finding worth by taking over someone else's life (codependent), or you are letting someone else define your worth for you (dependent). Either way, I thought I was helping him see Jesus, but in fact, I was blocking Jesus from doing the work that he wanted to do while hurting myself all the while.

In addition to extending the relationship to feel needed, I was too afraid to trust God with him. I didn't think that God could save him without me. I thought that I was the only one who could show him the love of Jesus. I boxed God in. I limited him to a God that could only work through me. Someone once told me something profound, "God can get tiny if you're not careful." I love that, but that isn't the God I know now. Jesus said it best. *"With man this is impossible, but with God all things are possible" (Matthew 9:26).* Eventually, I sought counsel, and my therapist told me to "let go and let God," as they say in the church. I cut off all communication with him. I allowed him to move on, and I created a space for God to work. I made space for someone new and healthy to come into my life and his. I still pray for him and that he will see the love of God in a big way, but it will be without me.

Though many verses speak of God's INCREDIBLY VAST power, the below encompass it beautifully:

Job 9: 4-10 "His wisdom is profound, his power is vast. Who has resisted him and come out unscathed? He moves mountains without their knowing it and overturns them in his anger. He shakes the earth from its place and makes its pillars tremble. He speaks to the sun and it does not shine; he seals off the light of the stars. He alone stretches out the heavens and treads on the waves of the sea. He is the Maker of the Bear and Orion, the Pleiades and the constellations of the south. He performs wonders that cannot be fathomed, miracles that cannot be counted."

Proverbs 3:5-6 "Trust in the Lord with all your heart and lean not on your own understanding; in all your ways submit to him, and he will make your paths straight.

So friend, learn to let go. You cannot fix anyone else, and you can't change anyone else. That is for God to worry about unless He has clearly and specifically told you to do something about it. Jesus doesn't want us to impose ourselves and take over someone's life in this way. While yes, Jesus sacrificed Himself for us, He didn't impose Himself on us. No, He died so that we could have the option to know Him, but He never forced that decision on us. He gave us authority and responsibility for our own lives. He didn't take it from us like I was trying to do with my ex.

Something to be cautious of is that codependency doesn't end with the relationship. It carries over into dating life as well. It affects your attraction to men and people in general. It is so SNEAKY. For example, say you were presented with two men: one who is tall, successful, kind, and loves Jesus and a man who is not who you envisioned at all but is a little wounded. Because of subconscious codependent patterns, you would probably choose the wounded one 9/10 times. It is this weird, subconscious phenomenon that sets you up for disaster. I am speaking out of experience here. So if you don't know why you are ending up in relationships with the same type of men, that could be why. But God wants so much more for us. So for you to pick a keeper in your next relationship, you need to address the core issue.

The core issue with codependency is that you are unconsciously finding your sense of worth in taking over someone else's life, or in the case of the dependent, you are unconsciously finding your worth in someone else. You find your sense of worth in being needed to an unhealthy degree. That is why when your ex finds someone else who can fill that need, it destroys your worth. You are no longer the sole caretaker of their life, or you were cast aside and deemed less worthy. Whether you are finding worth in "fixing" other people's lives or letting someone else define your worth for you, it is not sustainable. You need to find your worth in the one who has already deemed you worthy. Once you genuinely can grasp this concept, your "attraction" will begin to correct and shift towards the man God has for you.

Diving Deeper:

1. Do you identify with the codependent or the dependent? If so, why?

_____

_____

_____

_____

_____

2. What is one guardrail that you can put in place for your next relationship to ensure that you are neither the codependent nor the dependent?

_____

_____

_____

_____

_____

3. Are you afraid to let go and let God?

_____

_____

_____

_____

_____

4. Is there anything God told you specifically while reading this?

_____

_____

_____

_____

_____

PRAYER: God, show us where our true sense of worth comes from. Teach us that we cannot look to others and take what we can only get from you. As we learn more about you and healthy relationships, show us the boundaries that we need to protect our hearts and the hearts of those we love.

DAY 11

~~~~~~~~~~~~~~~~~~~

UNDERSTANDING ATTRACTION

♪

Song: Beauty for Ashes + You're
Good - UPPERROOM

Let's dig deeper into attraction, then. Many of us think that attraction is one-dimensional: based on looks. That was the only measure of attraction that I knew growing up. Maybe it was all those princess movies with the handsome prince who was the perfect height and had a muscular build and sharp features. What blew my mind was when I learned how attraction works and how it is multi-dimensional. If you are not aware of what you are naturally attracted to and why you will wind up always letting your attraction lead you in the wrong direction.

If you have listened to pastors talk about Christian dating, they warn the same thing. "It's not about looks. Attraction is a force that grows and is not always something that happens right away." I did not buy into that whenever I heard those sermons. It made me mad at the church. It felt like the church was telling me to settle. It made me angry at God, too, to the point where I found myself saying to God, "Looks are non-negotiable. I will not settle." The real reason I thought that was probably because I found a lot of worth in being in a relationship with a good-looking man, but it also stemmed from my lack of knowledge about the way attraction works. See, most articles that I've read on attraction will tell you how to make yourself more attractive, but they don't tell you why you are attracted to the type of people you date.

When I started to look into attraction further, I found this podcast from Ken Page called *Why We Get Attracted to the Wrong People*. LISTEN TO WHAT HE SAYS BECAUSE IT'S INSANE. He said that we are attracted to people who can hurt us in the same way our primary caregivers or other significant relationships hurt us when we were younger. I'll give you a loose example. Say my parents always implied that I was not good enough. The significant other that I would be attracted to would probably also do things that suggested that I was not good enough either.

Our psyche wants to get our significant other, who represents this love we have always wanted, to love us back to finally receive the love that we lacked as children. In doing this, there is a seed of knowing that there will be rejection, unavailability, disappointment or hurt in this relationship. Our subconscious goal is to get that person to finally love us right to repair the damage created from our primary relationships. Wild right? He said that it is called an **attraction of deprivation**. Look it up. This type of attraction makes us always end up feeling like we have to do something to finally win our partner's love, approval, and care. And it GRABS at us. He says that attractions of deprivation are essentially an **intermittent reward system**, which is the most compelling form of a reward system. It is this: you don't know when your reward will come because it happens sporadically. In this circumstance, the reward is love. You get doses of intimacy, love, or appreciation, but absolute unconditional love and acceptance never come. We don't want to leave the relationship because we don't want to miss out when the reward finally does come. We tend to think that the reward will be steady in the future. That is why there is that all-consuming feeling that we need that significant other's love and approval and that we cannot live without them. It is that codependent attraction of deprivation that makes us feel worthless without the acceptance of our loved one. He goes on to say that our early wiring tells us that this person is the key to salvation; they hold the key to real love. We subconsciously believe that choosing someone not like that is giving up on love, living a loveless existence. That is where I was!

Something we can do to correct this attraction is to surround ourselves with friends who remind us that this person is not good for us and remind us that there is better for us out there. As annoying as it is to hear that from friends, you need it. You need those friends who remind you that you can do so much better and that you aren't going to be ready for that right relationship if you keep dating this "type" of person. These friendships are **attractions of inspiration**: people who are kind, generous, honest, genuinely available, and consistent. So surround yourself with people who represent real consistent love and wean yourself away from negative relationships. The more time you spend around people who know your worth, the better you'll understand your worth, and the more likely the next relationship you get into is with someone who does too.

As I mentioned in previous sections of this devotional, I was attracted to wounded people who needed me. It was because I grew up in a household filled with wounded people who all needed me in some way. When my therapist told me that, I was mind blown. It all lined up perfectly. My problem wasn't that I didn't find nice guys attractive. It was that my psyche was seeking reparations from past wounds. It seemed that my attraction began to repair itself after realizing it and surrounding myself with people who love me no matter what.

In the Bible, the title for this section of scripture below is called "Life by the Spirit." I love that. Let's read Galatians 5:13-18:

"You, my brothers and sisters, were called to be free. But do not use your freedom to indulge the flesh; rather, serve one another humbly in love. For the entire law is fulfilled in keeping this one command: "Love your neighbor as yourself."[b] If you bite and devour each other, watch out or you will be destroyed by each other. So I say, walk by the Spirit, and you will not gratify the desires of the flesh. For the flesh desires what is contrary to the Spirit, and the Spirit what is contrary to the flesh. They are in conflict with each other so that you are not to do whatever[c] you want. But if you are led by the Spirit, you are not under the law."

Sometimes we feel like slaves to these attractions of deprivation, but Paul says that in Jesus, we are called to be free. Free from the bounds and weight of this world. Even more, he says that if we bite and devour each other, we will destroy each other. That is what many of my past relationships have looked like: destruction. It was probably more me than anything. So, as we learn to walk with the Spirit of God, He will change our desires to be contrary to what the "flesh" or world desires. The key to freedom in the kingdom of God is the Spirit, and we will talk more about this in a later chapter.

Diving Deeper:

1. Write out the most predominant characteristics of all the men you have been interested in or dated. Are there any common threads?

_____

_____

_____

_____

_____

2. Are there any common traits that you would attribute to either a primary caregiver or an influential person in your life?

_____

_____

_____

_____

3. Awareness is half of the battle. Write out a prayer and ask God to reveal further what is behind your attractions.

_____

_____

_____

_____

4. Is there anything God told you specifically while reading this?

_____

_____

_____

_____

PRAYER: Hey, God. How are you? We are just so excited to be in your presence today. You continue to break things off of us that we can't even see yet, and we are thankful. We want your best, but we need help. You can change hearts and lives. God, give us a distaste for any relationship that does not reflect you and your perfect love. We want to find a man that has your heart. One that acts, loves, and serves like you. We love you.

DAY 12

————⁓⁓∿᷂᷂᷂◦~◦⟨⟩◦~◦⟨⟩᷂᷂◦∿⁓⁓————

FINDING COMMUNITY

♪

Song: Holy Ground - Hillsong UNITED

When you are with your friends, I want you to do something for me. Look to your left and right and pay attention to who you spend your time with. Do you want to become more like them? If the answer is no, it is crucial for your growth to find an alternative community. You become like the top five people you spend the most time with. This is a touchy subject for some people. For people who have been through it emotionally or have not-so-great family lives, your friends are your family. I AM NOT SAYING TO ABANDON THESE PEOPLE OR TO JUDGE THEM. I am saying that while, yes, those relationships are such a beautiful thing and you should continue to love these people, it is vital that you find some form of Christ-centered community.

Have you ever looked into the first church ever created in Acts? It is nothing like our churches today. It didn't have a pastor who shared a message each week. It wasn't just a place you went to get fed the word, not talk to anyone, and leave right after. It was nothing like that. It was a place where Christians met to edify and encourage each other. Anyone who had an encouraging message could share what God has been doing in their life. It was a place to learn to hear God, receive, and understand His love. It was a place that took in the homeless, the needy, the outcasts and protected them. It was unlike any that we currently have today. We were made for community, and we were made for a community like this. The "church" as we know it today was not the vision. I think that is why the word "church" has such a negative connotation; we failed to make it a community. Instead, it is like a weekly class that may or may not be in line with the actual character of God. I am not trying to turn you away from the church in general. In fact, we are all together, one body, so they are a part of the kingdom of God. I just want to reframe your thinking regarding what church is. If you are meeting with a body of believers, being edified and uplifted, being poured into, and learning more about the beautiful character of our God, you are at church. It can also take place multiple times a week. It doesn't just have to be on Sundays. If you want to cook dinner for your friends and intentionally talk about the Lord, you have church.

Here is the deal, we are designed for community. We need it. I think the overall hierarchical structure of our church today isn't working. Still, it is a great place to find a community. I have joined a couple of small groups throughout my life. Some have worked, and some have not. It is very much a trial and error process. Some groups might be filled with what you might consider "holier than thou" Christians who may have even turned you away from the church, but some are filled with people who are following Jesus with their whole hearts. Those are the groups that can change the course of your life. Honestly there is always something to learn from the holier than thou" Christians even if they make you mad. Even Jesus said to listen to what the Pharisees say, just don't do what they do, which was practice hypocrisy (Matthew 23:1-3). We need a community of believers walking alongside us, encouraging us in our faith, praying for us, lifting us when we are down, and loving us through our life.

I told my best friend about the growth I experienced from my small group, and she said that it wasn't appealing to her to join a group like that. She said she didn't want to feel judged or spend time with boring people. And if you grew up in the church, that is VALID. I did, too. But, that is not the community that I am talking about. I am talking about a community that puts Christ first and foremost. And when you find people that do, they breathe life into you. You can feel the kingdom of heaven in their midst. To grow spiritually, you need your brothers and sisters in Christ. You need community.

Let me tell you about my last small group that changed my life. After my last breakup, I was so broken. I wanted a relationship with God but couldn't figure out my next step. Luckily, my brother encouraged me to find a group of Christian girls to do Bible Study with. I found a great one just by asking around. This group was incredible. Something so powerful would happen when we gathered, like a thin space of heaven entered the room. They spoke truth in my life when good friends might have been afraid to step on my toes. They taught and guided me, but best of all, they came alongside me and prayed for me. I found myself sharing freely about things I NEVER thought I would tell anyone, and you know what? They didn't treat me any differently, judge me, or pity me but loved me and admired me more for it. These are the truest attractions of inspiration. It is vital that you are shown that no matter what, you are loved. That group ended, and now I have a new community that I gather with that breathes a lot of life into me. We all have different thoughts on theology and following Christ, but we all love each other and work towards serving and loving everyone we meet.

SO DO IT. FIND YOUR GROUP. LOVE THEM AND CHERISH THEIR EXISTENCE. It might be difficult and awkward at first, but it is so rewarding. The growth you will experience just by taking this one step is unbelievable. We have laughed, cried, and struggled to stay on the straight and narrow, but we did it together. I know you will find a similar situation if you reach out and try.

Connect with your local church if you don't know where to find one. Most churches have some form of a small group.

> *Ephesians 4: 2-16 says, " Be completely humble and gentle; be patient, bearing with one another in love. Make every effort to keep the unity of the in Spirit through the bond of peace. There is one body and one Spirit, just as you were called to one hope when you were called; one Lord, one faith, one baptism; one God and Father of all, who is over all and through all and in all."Until we all reach unity in the faith and in the knowledge of the Son of God and become mature, attaining to the whole measure of the fullness of Christ. Then we will no longer be infants, tossed back and forth by the waves, and blown here and there by every wind of teaching and by the cunning and craftiness of people in their deceitful scheming. Instead, speaking the truth in love, we will grow to become in every respect the mature body of him who is the head, that is, Christ. From him the whole body, joined and held together by every supporting ligament, grows and builds itself up in love, as each part does its work."*
>
> *Proverbs 13:20 says, "Walk with the wise and become wise, for a companion of fools suffers harm."*
>
> *Proverbs 27:17 says, "As iron sharpens iron, so one person sharpens another."*
>
> *1 Corinthians 15:33 says, "Do not be misled: 'Bad company corrupts good character.'"*

We were made to be one body in a community with other

believers. That is how you grow in your relationship with Christ. You flourish with the body. You were made to receive love from God and man to pour back your love into God and man. A community like this keeps you from wavering, and it puts you on a steady path. I know it can be intimidating, especially if you are trying to form a group, but it is so life-changing. And what is even more exciting is Jesus says HE IS THERE. "Where two or three gather in my name, there I am with them (Matt 18:20)." He is there holding your hand while you walk down this path, encouraging you, and whispering that He loves you and is so proud of you.

My friend Jess told me something really sweet about taking these trial and error steps toward God. She said, "it is like a father watching his child take a step for the first time. If the child falls, does the father criticize his child for trying? No, the father is on his feet dancing, celebrating, and screaming, 'That is my girl! Isn't she incredible?'" God is guiding you on your path. He is proud of you for taking a step. Don't let the enemy tell you otherwise.

Diving Deeper:

1. Do you believe that you are who you spend your time with? Why?

   _____

   _____

   _____

   _____

   _____

2. Are you afraid to get to know other Christians? Why?

   _____

   _____

   _____

_____

_____

3. Make a list of churches, groups, and people that you can reach
    out to to begin the process of finding community and contact
    at least 1.

_____

_____

_____

_____

_____

4. Is there anything God told you specifically while reading this?

_____

_____

_____

_____

_____

PRAYER: God, we know how important the body is to our growth
and the world's. Whether we are in a good community now or are
looking for one, I pray that you put people in our path this week,
this month, this year even that we can learn from. People that will
further teach us about you. We want the community that you intend
for us to have. We pray that people looking for community find it
and that if we can help bring one together, you will use us to do
so. Help us push past the uncomfortable to further your kingdom.

DAY 13

———— ∿◦ᴄ᷒ᴇᴠᴏᴄ᷒ᴇᴏ∿ ————

TIME OUT

♪

Song: Eyes on You - Mosaic MSC

This passage may not be for everyone, but this message is probably for you if it feels like I am talking to you. I will give you some advice that may seem religious at first but saved me a lot of time and heartbreak and might save you some, especially if you empathize with any of the above passages. If you are familiar with any of Andy Stanley's love, sex, and dating sermons, you have probably heard this advice before, and you've probably hated it. BUT here we go… Take a timeout from the dating scene. It might sound like I am trying to impose more rules on you, but this is just a suggestion.

If you opt-in, I would advise setting a specific timeline with an end date, like six months. You need a timeline, or you could meet someone great and break your commitment to not date. I know it sounds scary, especially since I know about the aforementioned time clock. BUT, this is SO IMPORTANT and will probably save you some time and heartbreak.

Why on earth would you do this? First and foremost, it creates an opportunity for you to get to know men as friends authentically.

If you know that you cannot date at the moment, you will not fixate on every attractive guy you meet and the potential of romance. Left unfixed, that constant searching creates a pattern you can carry into a relationship. I've known some incredible women who looked for a man for a long time, and when they finally met a good one, they ended up being dissatisfied because they were still looking at every man they met through the lens of a potential better romance. Secondly, creating mental space by blocking out thoughts of men allows God room to show you his great love for you and reawaken desires and dreams. I grew up thinking it would be so cool to write my story one day, and God re-awakened that desire in my time off from dating. Lastly, it gives you time to reflect on the type of man you've previously dated and the type of man you want to marry. This is important because you play a pretty significant role in choosing the person you want to spend the rest of your life with. And that is a LONG time to spend with just one person, so you should take some time beforehand to think about what you want.

I am not giving you this advice without taking it myself. When I started writing this, I was in this season, and while it was hard, I had never felt such deep love from God before in my life. I did get lonely, but learning to run to God to quiet that ache of loneliness is how you train yourself for the rest of your life; because guess what? You can feel lonely, even in a relationship or a marriage. We will dive deeper into loneliness in a later section.

I've taken a timeout from dating twice in my life. The first time was not so good. It was not healing whatsoever. But the second was my most cherished season of life thus far. What is the difference, you ask? Let me tell you about it.

My first timeout from the dating scene was in college, and I was going out all the time… It turns out "I am not interested in dating right now" is a pickup line for a girl in a college town. While the premise of not dating was good, my focus was way off. I listened to Andy's sermon and thought that my husband would just magically appear if I took a six-month hiatus from dating.

My focus was still on finding a husband rather than healing my wounds and view of God.

This time around was different. I surrounded myself with an incredible community, podcasts, scriptures, books, music, etc. (we will get into these tactics further on), and gave space for the Lord to speak to me, and He spoke to me more clearly in that season than ever before. While I still hoped for a husband, I focused on Jesus. Here is some life advice, never take your focus off God. The minute your focus changes, you sink. I took that advice from Matthew 14:25-33. Let's read it:

> "Shortly before dawn Jesus went out to them, walking on the lake. When the disciples saw him walking on the lake, they were terrified. "It's a ghost," they said, and cried out in fear. But Jesus immediately said to them: "Take courage! It is I. Don't be afraid." "Lord, if it's you," Peter replied, "tell me to come to you on the water." "Come," he said. Then Peter got down out of the boat, walked on the water and came toward Jesus. But when he saw the wind, he was afraid and, beginning to sink, cried out, "Lord, save me!" Immediately Jesus reached out his hand and caught him. "You of little faith," he said, "why did you doubt?" And when they climbed into the boat, the wind died down. Then those who were in the boat worshiped him, saying, "Truly you are the Son of God."

When we lock eyes with Jesus, suddenly the impossible becomes possible, but when we look at our circumstances, we begin to sink. Luckily Jesus is there to grab us. That is the best analogy for this season of life. Do not focus on your circumstances, instead lock eyes with Jesus.

Once again, I KNOW TAKING A TIME OUT IS SCARY and seems counterproductive. What if you miss your husband? What if you get asked out on a date by a nice Christian guy? Are you really supposed to say no to that? Yes. If this is the guy you will want to potentially marry, look at it as his first test. If he understands you want to work on yourself and get closer to the Lord, and he respects your boundaries, that is a good sign that he might be a good man to date.

If you choose to take this time out, here are some scriptures to put all over your room and/or bathroom that help you keep that focus:

> *Psalm 27:13-14: "I believe that I shall look[a] upon the goodness of the Lord in the land of the living! Wait for the Lord; be strong, and let your heart take courage; wait for the Lord!"*

> *Isaiah 40:31 "but they who wait for the Lord shall renew their strength; they shall mount up with wings like eagles; they shall run and not be weary; they shall walk and not faint."*

> *Lamentations 3:25 "The Lord is good to those who wait for him, to the soul who seeks him."*

> *Isaiah 30:18 "Therefore the Lord waits to be gracious to you, and therefore he exalts himself to show mercy to you. For the Lord is a God of justice; blessed are all those who wait for him."*

> *Micah 7:7 "But as for me, I will look to the Lord; I will wait for the God of my salvation; my God will hear me."*

So wait on God. Let Him heal your heart during this time. Let Him show you the plans that He has for you. I know that they aren't small. God didn't create each of us thinking that all we were going to do in this life was go to college, get married, have kids, and that's it. No, He created us holy and set apart: world changers, life-givers, and vessels to restore the world through Jesus. That is no small task. Paul even talks about the great work that can be done while in singleness and why it is harder to do the Lord's work while married in 1 Corinthians 7:28, 32, 35

> *"But those who marry will face many troubles in this life, and I want to spare you this… An unmarried woman is concerned about the Lord's affairs: Her aim is to be devoted to the Lord in both body and spirit. But a married woman is concerned about the affairs of this world—how she can please her husband… I am saying this for your own good, not to restrict you, but that you may live in a right way in undivided devotion to the Lord."*

I don't mention that to tell you that you should never want to marry because God gave most of us the desire to be married. In fact, I believe that God wants that for us. He created marriage, and that was before the fall! He wants to give you good gifts. I am saying this because, in this single season, you are (as a single person) able to do far more in total devotion to God than in a marriage where you need to be concerned about your husband. So, take this time out for yourself. Let God heal you, and let Him show you the grandiose plans He has for you.

Diving Deeper:

1. What are some of the best parts of your single season?

    _____

    _____

_____

_____

_____

2. What oppression in this world breaks your heart?

_____

_____

_____

_____

_____

3. What are your fears about devoting a certain amount of time to just focusing on God? Tell Him.

_____

_____

_____

_____

_____

4. Is there anything God told you specifically while reading this?

_____

_____

_____

_____

PRAYER: God, I pray that if any of these words were not helpful for this reader, that the words fall dead. But if this is the right step for them, you lightly convict their hearts. I pray that you give them excitement about this opportunity to focus on you and that you speak clearly to them during this time. I pray that any thoughts or anything that tries to dissuade them from this opportunity that you quiet them. This is all for you, Jesus.

DAY 14

———❦———

WHAT'S THE POINT?

♪

Song: Voice of God - Dante Bowe,
Steffany Gretzinger, Chandler Moore

During the midst of a difficult time, it is common to hear, "I'm praying for you." Right? And not just from your Christian or religious communities, but even from non-religious friends. I always appreciate it, of course, because I know the power of prayer, but it surprises me. Why would people say they were praying for me if they didn't believe in a higher power? I think it has to come from the fact that prayer, in itself, is a selfless act that shows that you are taking time out of your life to think about someone else and at least try to change the outcome of a situation out of your control.

Prior to jumping back into my relationship with God, all I did to invest in our relationship was occasionally pray. But recently, I realized that I had stopped praying. I think that as my trust in Jesus grew, I just assumed God was working everything together for my good, so why did I need to ask Him for anything? Right? What is the point of prayer if God knows the outcome? Can we change the outcome of a situation just by praying? How does that even work? It wasn't until I began to dig into the why behind prayer that I realized its importance and how my relationship with God was waning because of the lack of it. There is evidence to support that prayer does affect the outcome of situations in the Bible. So, if you've reached a point along your singleness journey where you think praying is pointless and God doesn't hear you, I will attempt to change your perspective and encourage you to keep praying.

If we take it back to the story of Moses and the exodus from Egypt, we find an incredible example of the power of prayer in the Bible. Exodus 32:7-14 tells us that God's wrath burned against the Israelites for turning to other gods. Moses pleads with the Lord on behalf of the Israelites:

> *"Lord, why does Your wrath burn hot against Your people whom You have brought out of the land of Egypt with great power and with a mighty hand? 12 Why should the Egyptians speak, and say, 'He brought them out to harm them, to kill them in the mountains, and to consume them from the face of the earth'? Turn from Your fierce wrath, and relent from this harm to Your people. 13 Remember Abraham, Isaac, and Israel, Your servants, to whom You swore by Your own self, and said to them, 'I will multiply your descendants as the stars of heaven; and all this land that I have spoken of I give to your descendants, and they shall inherit it forever.' 14 So the Lord relented from the harm which He said He would do to His people (Exodus 32: 11-14)."*

It's easy to get caught up in God's wrath here, but let's focus on the incredible fact that Moses, a HUMAN, ministered to the Lord, reminded Him of his character, and changed His mind with a prayer. *[Side note if you want to learn about God's wrath, listen to BEMA episode*

17]. That is powerful. It is easy to compare ourselves with Moses and think, "God loved him more. I wouldn't have the same pull with God." That isn't the case at all. God loves us just as much. You have just as much potential to change the world as Moses. He listens to us just as intently as He did with Moses. He wants us to ask Him for things. Doesn't that seem weird, though? Why? And if He does, why does it appear like He never answers our prayers?

Remember, God frames Himself as a father and not just a father but a good father. Let's talk about asking our dad for things. Tim Macke explained this ever so beautifully in one of his podcasts. He talks about how when we are young, like just learning to talk, our relationship with our parents is pretty much solely asking for things. For example, my nephew is almost a year old. The only way he can communicate is by asking for things he wants. My sister-in-law and my brother don't get mad at that. They don't punish him for asking for food or water. In fact, they encourage him to ask for more. It's the way their relationship was meant to be for the moment. They love being able to provide for him. God framed himself as a father who will and wants to provide.

If God wants us to ask Him for things, why does He never seem to answer our prayers or say yes to them? Did you ever ask your dad to eat dessert for every meal when you were young? It is as simple as this: our understanding of the world was limited when we were younger. We saw ice cream and thought it was good. We couldn't possibly comprehend the actual dangers of eating ice cream for every meal, how it would possibly give us diabetes, and we wouldn't get as much protein and vitamins as we needed (no matter what the Mayfield ice cream boxes say). Our understanding was limited, but guess who knew that it wouldn't turn out so well if we ate that way? Our dad. Because our dad had more knowledge than us, He could see outcomes that our limited, tiny minds couldn't even fathom. I think that God works like that. When we pray and ask our father for things, He listens, but sometimes He does not say yes because of the potential outcomes that a yes would bring. Something that we think is good might just look good right now, but we can never actually know how it would impact us in the long term.

I was recently listening to a BEMA podcast, and God confirmed to me again why He doesn't tell us His plan when we ask Him. He confirmed it by using the story of Abraham's life. Near the beginning of Abraham's story, God tells him that He will make Abraham a great nation. Through context clues and the study of the Hebrew language, you are supposed to gather that Abraham thinks his great nation will come through his nephew, Lot, because Abraham's wife Sarah couldn't conceive. Lot leaves Abraham, and we find Abraham (previously known as Abram) questioning how God will make him a great nation when it seems impossible.

> *"**But Abram said**, 'Sovereign Lord, what can you give me since I remain childless and the one who will inherit my estate is Eliezer of Damascus?' **And Abram said**, 'You have given me no children; so a servant in my household will be my heir (Genesis 15:2-3).'"*

In the Hebrew language, when a person in a conversation is talking and their text is broken up by an additional "And _ said." you are supposed to infer that these are two separate conversations. For example, in the above passage, "And Abram said,'" starts a new conversation with God. The Hebrews teach that we aren't to assume the length of time between conversations. It could've been hours or weeks. Why am I teaching you this seemingly useless Hebraic literary tool? By the author writing this passage in this way, we can conclude that God did not want to tell Abraham the plan. Why is that? Because God knew Abraham would mess it up if He told him. But after multiple prayers, God ends up giving him part of the plan:

> *Then the word of the Lord came to him: "This man will not be your heir, but a son who is your own flesh and blood will be your heir (Genesis 15:4)."*

Guess what happened next? Abraham messed it up. He took matters into his own hands to attempt to fulfill God's plan by sleeping with Hagar. Abraham could have never imagined God's initial plan would be so much greater. God planned for Sarah to conceive a child even though she was infertile. How could Abraham have guessed that? It seems ludicrous and impossible, but that is God. He is wild and surprising and more incredible than we can ever imagine. So when we pray and don't receive a response, maybe it is because God is working together something more fantastical and surprising than we can imagine. He is working together something beautiful that we deem impossible, but out of his glorious love for us, He makes a way.

There is another insane example of God not answering a prayer in the Bible that blows my mind to this day. When Jesus, who is one with God, is in the garden of Gethsemane, He asks God for another way for His will to be done. Jesus said, *"My Father, if it is not possible for this cup to be taken away unless I drink it, may your will be done* (Matthew 26:42)." God didn't take the cup from him. Why? Because God wanted us. He wanted to restore the relationship that was broken over sin. Jesus dying in the way that He did was the best way.

Relationship is the key to prayer. Prayer is just that, being in relationship with God. That is epic. It doesn't even seem natural that the God who created the sun, moon, stars, tide, ocean, and all living creatures wants us to spend time with Him and ask Him for things. And because God wants us to ask Him for things, it is safe to say that we could be missing out on blessings because we aren't asking. Jesus said to ask God for things **because** He already knows what you need (Matthew 6:8). He didn't say ask God to let Him know what you need. No, ask God, especially because He knows what you need, and He wants to give you good things. He wants that relationship with you.

1 John 5:14-15 "This is the confidence we have in approaching God: that if we ask anything according to his will, he hears us. And if we know that he hears us--whatever we ask--we know that we have what we asked of him."

What is even more foundational than all of that is learning to hear God's voice. God is always speaking to us. Sometimes it is utterly obvious, but other times, it is just an impression that you have that takes time to decipher. If you want to learn to hear his voice, there are two books I will recommend later in the devotional that are so great. The more time you carve out and sit with God, and the more you learn His thoughts and character from scripture, the more you can begin to hear and decipher His voice. It took me a long time to tune into God's frequency. It took a lot of sitting, praying, and being around people who could help me figure it out, but I am so thankful I did.

So ask. Pray. Seek. Knock. He is listening. He cares, and He hears you.

Diving Deeper:

1. What have you been praying for that seems too impossible for God to handle?

    _____

    _____

    _____

    _____

    _____

2. 7Ask God to show you how He is working in these prayers.

_____

_____

_____

_____

_____

3. Is there anything God told you specifically while reading this?

_____

_____

_____

_____

_____

PRAYER: What a blessing it is to be able to talk to you. We want to hear your voice more clearly. This is an individual journey for this reader. Teach them how personal your relationship with them is. It is one of a kind.

--- I will let you take it from here.

DAY 15

HARMFUL COPING MECHANISMS

♪

Song: King of My Heart - Stefanie Gretzinger

A friend once told me that when you quit a bad habit, you just replace it with a new one. This is due to our need/want to fill that nagging feeling in our souls that only our creator can fill. In our case, our past relationship was probably similar to a bad habit, and maybe you even picked a few actual bad habits from it. When we nixed that relationship, we left a massive hole in our life and subconsciously started searching for a fill. I will go ahead and list a few that I struggled with. These "habits" are not bad on their own, but when used to fill the hole in our hearts, they can be harmful. This next section could be somewhat controversial, so buckle up, hang on to your hats, hearts, or whatever because this will be a little bumpy.

I will go through a few worldly coping mechanisms or "habits" that are very prevalent and will lead you, inevitably, to some form of emptiness. I am only going through this as a warning, not a judgment. I just want the very best for you. Most of this is based on personal experience, so let's dig in:

Social Media

In an ideal world, my advice would be to give it up altogether. It is so addicting, and it automatically puts us in a comparison mindset. It keeps us in the trenches of hurt. However, this may not be an option for you. So, it might be a good idea to put some guardrails in place. When my ex and I broke up, the first thing I did was block him from all social platforms. Then I muted everyone I followed who could potentially post something with him. I needed time and space to heal. I know it was kind of extreme, but knowing myself and knowing what would trigger me to fall into harmful mental patterns, I did it. Your trigger might not be your ex, but you know the things when you see them. In addition to pruning your feed, following scripture accounts is helpful. The random pops of scripture might help get you out of the comparison mind trap. Sometimes the Lord will speak to me through them as well. Maybe even try fasting social media for a month or so to see what life is like without it. Trust me, there is peace and realization at the end of that tunnel.

> *Colossians 3:1-3 Since, then, you have been raised with Christ, set your hearts on things above, where Christ is seated at the right hand of God. Set your minds on things above, not on earthly things. For you died, and your life is now hidden with Christ in God.*

Drinking

If you enjoy drinking, I am with you, but speaking from experience, using it to cope can bring a lot of harm. Scientifically, alcohol is a depressant, meaning simply that it messes with your brain chemicals. The short explanation is that while you are drinking, your brain overproduces GABA (the relaxing brain chemical) and decreases glutamate production (the anxiety brain chemical), which is why you feel so good. As soon as you wake up from a night of drinking, your brain flips the switch and stops producing GABA and begins to overproduce glutamate. Which in turn gives you the ever so terrifying "scaries." Plus, the likelihood of you doing something that you might not do sober increases 10-fold. I found that when I was healing and drinking all of the time, I did things that set me back and put me in complicated circumstances. So maybe put together another list of guard rails: block people you tend to run to for comfort (i.e., exes) on text and social or ask for trustworthy friends to keep you accountable. If you ask someone to hold you accountable, let them keep you accountable, and don't let shame cover you when they do. Once again, I am not telling you to stop drinking. I am telling you to stop using it to cope. As the "fun Christians" say, "Even Jesus drank wine." BUT if you are using it to fill a hole in your heart, you will spend a lot of time in heart-wrenching pain. That breaks my heart to think about for you because, as I said, I walked through it, and it HURT.

Shopping

As women in a world full of bloggers and media, we prioritize what we wear and how we look. While I know it is fun to shop and put together outfits, it is another distraction from something deeper. I used to be a buyer for a women's clothing store and a model. I was living for pictures and clothing. I wore, what I thought, were the cutest clothes we sold at our stores. I bi-annually studied fashion week like my life depended on knowing what was going to be "in." And guess what? Since social media developed, fashion trends change way more frequently than seasonally. It Is exhausting to try to be "in." For me, it was more than just getting a compliment on my outfit; it was an identity issue. I was a "buyer." If I didn't dress the part, I thought people would think I was unqualified or that I must not be good at my job. I also took a lot of pride in being fashionable. I had to step back recently and detach that identity from myself and do a shopping fast. Jesus says this, which is almost a little too poignant to what I'm talking about:

> *Matthew 6: 28-33 "And why do you worry about clothes? See how the flowers of the field grow. They do not labor or spin. Yet I tell you that not even Solomon in all his splendor was dressed like one of these. If that is how God clothes the grass of the field, which is here today and tomorrow is thrown into the fire, will he not much more clothe you—you of little faith? So do not worry, saying, 'What shall we eat?' or 'What shall we drink?' or 'What shall we wear?' For the pagans run after all these things, and your heavenly Father knows that you need them. But seek first his kingdom and his righteousness, and all these things will be given to you as well."*

Meaningless Sex

Before I start this. I just want you to know that you are not to feel shame here. Rather the point is to convince you that YOU (not your body) are INFINITELY VALUABLE and ultra-rare. So if while you are reading this, you start to feel shame…. I DECLARE SHAME OFF OF YOU. That is just the enemy trying to get you to abandon this healing path that you are on.

The church has done irreparable damage in the conversation of sex. I apologize on behalf of the Christian community. Because the church condemns sex outside of marriage so harshly, no one wants to hear anything new they have to say about the subject matter. And I am with everyone here. I think if the church hadn't used shame and sin as the reason not to have sex, I might have waited a little bit longer. I don't want to sit here and have this sex talk with you, but I do want to tell you your value is not in your body.

Our world perceives relationships as a value exchange on multiple levels. For a large portion of the female population, the value exchange is thought of as: getting protection, love, acceptance, and worth from a man, and they, in turn, receive sex. The majority of our perceived value lies in the fact that we can provide sex. Why? Maybe it's the long-standing history of men being able to pay for sex. Perhaps it's the billion-dollar industry of porn. Maybe it's Hollywood. Whatever the case, we have to believe that we are more than what our body brings to the table.

We have for far too long been told not to use our brains but to use our bodies instead. That's why you should see if you are compatible, interested in the same things, etc., before having sex. You have a brain. You have thoughts, opinions, insight, stories. Our value doesn't derive from those things, either. God has already called us worthy. Our value in His kingdom is infinite. He says that you are inherently valuable. You are worth a guy opening a car door for you. You are worth getting to know and getting spoiled without offering anything in return. You are worth a man giving you a lifelong commitment before having sex. You are worth being discovered and pursued over a long period of time. You are worth the wait. It seems impossible for us to believe that, and even if we do, it doesn't matter because we also crave intimacy from sex. That, mixed with the fact that we feel our value comes from our bodies, makes the phrase, "you should wait until you are married to have sex" the most ridiculous phrase ever. It does. It sounds ludicrous. As much as I think it's in your best interest to wait to have sex, it doesn't generally happen that way.

To be completely vulnerable, I'll tell you a bit of my story. I am convinced that the enemy has used (a form of) sex for generations to bring emptiness into our hearts. I went through a phase of MAJOR brokenness fueled by the partial lie that sex was power over men. More than that, I thought that if I said I didn't want a relationship and all I wanted was sex (AKA using someone), I had the upper hand. That is a prevalent thought in the young adult world. Use people and don't get your heart involved to protect yourself, and maybe it will turn into something more. It was the most terrible, lonely, detrimental season of my life. I was a tornado of hurt just gathering, destroying, and tossing a few young men who came into my path. These men were probably put into my path to restore their self-worth, call them higher, build them up, and show them the love of Jesus, but instead, I did the exact opposite. And even worse, the frail ladybug-sized piece of self-worth that I had before that season was wiped out and thrown into oblivion. I was an empty shell of a person. So, my warning is this: it will not fill you, and in your quest for it to, you can hurt others and yourself. That hit of intimacy causes pain that you can't see. Proverbs 4:23 says, "Above all else, guard your heart, for everything you do flows from it." Your heart is beautiful. Your life is of the highest value. Your personality and love are forces to be reckoned with. You are RARE.

The Perfect Body

My personal least favorite quote of all time is from Kate Moss. "Nothing tastes as good as skinny feels." That phrase consistently lived in the back of my head in my short-lived career as a professional model. My agent gave me size goals that I needed to work toward to get booked. I took it to the extreme. I worked out almost every day (if not twice a day), and I restricted my caloric intake to ~1000 calories a day. Do you know who that is okay for? 6-year-old girls. But I was obsessed. Weight was my sole focus. And guess what? When I eventually got down to the "correct" size, it wasn't enough for me. I never felt in shape enough. I knew that there were models way skinnier than myself, and I wanted to be the smallest of them all. It wasn't until I stopped modeling that my relationship with food and exercise started to repair. Let me tell you, not once in Proverbs 31 does it say that a woman of worth is worthy because she is skinny. NO, this is a dead-end. Instead, the Bible compares our body to the temple. If you aren't familiar with ancient Jewish history, the temple is a big deal. It was beautiful, and it was designed ornately, with the purpose being to house the spirit of God (1 Kings 6). Same with us. God took care in creating us with the purpose that we would house His Spirit within us. Each part of our bodies is purposefully designed. The enemy knows that and wants you to be mad at God for that. Thankfully, I know now that I have a choice to let my mind think those thoughts. I will choose to bring my thoughts back to the fact that I am fearfully and wonderfully made.

> *Song of Solomon 4:7 "My darling, everything about you is beautiful, and there is nothing at all wrong with you."*

> *Psalm 45:11a "Let the king be enthralled by your beauty."*

Career

When I graduated college, I became a buyer for a medium-sized chain of women's clothing boutiques. That was it for me. I fell in love with my job. It consumed me and became a part of my identity. I had the job that so many others wanted. I got to shop for a living. I learned that it was not all I cracked it up to be very early on. I was working long hours, making no money, exhausted, and was pushed to my limits. I was constantly told that my work was never good enough, and I was made to feel like I never measured up day in and day out. I felt worthless, but through that, God quickly told me my value is not what I produce, achieve, or how much I make.

> *1 Peter 1:18-20 "For you know that it was not with perishable things such as silver or gold that you were redeemed from the empty way of life handed down to you from your ancestors, but with the precious blood of Christ, a lamb without blemish or defect. He*

was chosen before the creation of the world, but was revealed in these last times for your sake."

There are endless worldly coping mechanisms that you could use to fill your God-sized hole: drugs, Netflix binging, Instagram, eating, new relationships, money, etc., but I want to caution you that none of them will fill you. I have tried all of them. I felt like a modern-day King Solomon on my quest for finding meaning in the world in the wrong ways. If you don't know about King Solomon, you should read his story.

He tried the exact same thing in the Old Testament. In the book of Ecclesiastes, we find Solomon's documentation on his quest to find fulfillment in worldly things apart from God. He wanted wisdom, and God gave it to him. He became the wisest king to rule up until that point, but It wasn't enough. He tried wealth, career, power, sex, drinking, artistic entertainment, multiple wives (700 to be exact), and more. Eventually, all avenues of potential fulfilment lead to "hevel" (original Hebrew language), which means "vain", "empty", "meaningless", "temporary", "transitory", or "fleeting." King Solomon came to the eventual conclusion that:

Ecclesiastes 12: 13-14 "...here is the conclusion of the matter: Fear God and keep his commandments..."

That's insane, right? He says that keeping God's commandments is better than everything listed above. Keeping God's commands is better than money? Better than marriage? Better than power? Something I want to point out is that Solomon lived under the Old Covenant. The Old Covenant said that in exchange for the Israelites abiding by the Ten Commandments and the laws in Leviticus, they would be God's chosen people, they would prosper, and they would be protected. We live under the New Covenant that says that all we have to do to be God's chosen people is change our minds and believe that because Jesus died for us, we are redeemed. Our fulfillment is found in being in relationship with God.

If you don't take Him at his word, take me at mine. As I have gone on my journey, I can tell you that I have found complete agreement with him, and many others have as well. Once again, it's not that if we follow all of God's commandments, we will feel complete. That is not what Solomon is saying. He is saying that if we live in constant communion with God, abiding in his love and pouring it out to other people, we will be full. That is the great commandment.

> *"'Teacher, which is the greatest commandment in the Law?' Jesus replied: "'Love the Lord your God with all your heart and with all your soul and with all your mind.' This is the first and greatest commandment. And the second is like it: 'Love your neighbor as yourself.' All the Law and the Prophets hang on these two commandments (Matthew 22:36-40)."*

When we get that, we will realize that nothing can fill our hearts except the one we were created for. As I said before, this is possible, true fulfillment from God. It is the ONLY fulfillment that will sustain long after your life is over on this earth.

Dive Deeper:

1. Reflect on your life for a minute. What have you chased in your life to fill you?

   _____

   _____

   _____

   _____

   _____

2. What evidence supports that it will fulfill you? Is the source reliable?

    _____

    _____

    _____

    _____

    _____

3. Is there anything God told you specifically while reading this?

    _____

    _____

    _____

    _____

    _____

PRAYER: I want to end this time with you, father, by saying that we need your help. We want coping mechanisms that bring long-term joy instead of long-term unfulfillment. We know that we are not going to do this all right by any means, and we are grateful that you love us exactly where we are anyways, but we want more of you. If there was any shame felt during this time, please get rid of it. If there was any conviction, please lovingly and patiently help us lean into it. You are the only one who can tell us, in your timing, what we need to do to heal, and we trust you to do so. Help us not jump in front of you and do this on our own strength. We need yours. Thank you that you are so good. WE LOVE YOU SO MUCH.

DAY 16

COMPARISON

♪

Song: Sing His Praise Again (Oh My Soul) - Bethel Music, Jenn Johnson

Comparison is the thief of joy. We've all heard this before. This topic is played out, so I will try not to go into the do's and don'ts of comparison and just talk about some things that I have learned working through this. My comparison struggles might look different than yours, but as single women, we probably all compare our lives to peers who are getting married and having children. Let me remind you what you already know: pictures are not reality. They aren't even close. Most people will not pick up their phones to post about their struggles, fights, addictions, or heartaches. I follow this blogger who I thought had it all: she had a perfect life, marriage, and family. One day out of the blue, she posted about her and her husband getting a divorce. I was heartbroken for them. Their marriage seemed perfect. Truth be told, things were going on behind the scenes that were not so picture-perfect. They couldn't make it work anymore. I hate using that example because I wouldn't want any blogger who goes through a divorce to read this and think that they are being shamed. Shame off! I am just trying to get across that social media is just a one-sided view of our lives. It is the good and beautiful, not the real and raw. To compare your life to something that might not truly exist is just dangerous.

As I previously mentioned, Paul harped on how difficult it is to be married. That is the reality. It is harder to fulfill your purpose in marriage than to do it while single. And I know you are thinking that I am insane in saying that, but it is true. Think about being married for 50 years. What happens when you get tired of that person? What happens when you get into huge fights? What happens if they change? What happens when the money runs out? You have to think about someone else all of the time. And can you imagine having kids on top of that?

In addition to comparing where we are in our lives with others, we also compare our looks with the Instagram world. We've completely got it all wrong, haven't we? We let society's ever-changing standards define how we perceive our beauty. With all of these new face filters allowing us to see what we could look like with oodles of plastic surgery, we are a society morphing our faces and bodies to achieve an unrealistic standard that will inevitably change again in a few years. And it is never enough. If you start with a nose job (like I did), you want fillers, botox, and implants. It never ends. It is chasing the wind, chasing something you cannot grasp: satisfaction through beautification.

Something I know the enemy does is glorify the changing of outward appearance as a solution to the emptiness in our souls. He says, "the nagging will stop once you alter your appearance. You'll feel completely satisfied when you are pretty enough, thin enough, symmetrical enough." In our day and age, he has removed the stigma from altering our outward appearance but heavied it for altering our inward appearance. What I mean by that is this... In our society, it is accepted and even encouraged to spend $1,000+ on plastic surgery, but not usually encouraged or accepted to spend $1,000 on therapy. In my experience, most people accept that others go to a counselor, but they won't go themselves. It is almost like a sign of weakness to some people or, when mentioned, met with concern or awkwardness. I think it is because the enemy knows the good of counseling. A LOT of good comes from it if you have a counselor who is a good fit for you. The enemy builds that stigma towards counseling. He creates an adverse reaction to it because if he didn't and we all were to truly work through our issues, the world would look a lot more like Jesus. If you look at all of the external conflicts in the world and the people involved, you can usually see that it is just a spillover of their internal conflict.

Everyone I know in the world is wounded. That is the sad reality of sin entering the world. It is just how they tend to the wounds that determine their external outpour. A friend said that an internal injury is similar to a physical injury. If you fall and get a cut, it's essential to clean the wound and cover it to heal correctly. The cleaning of the wound hurts almost worse than getting the wound, but once it is dressed, it can heal and become a part of your story. If you don't clean and dress your wound, it will slowly worsen and become infected.

Another very unusual form of comparison that you might encounter on this journey with God is comparing your walk with God to others. As an overview of your time with God, you will have highs and lows. It is funny because lows usually bring on my highs with God. I will feel God and hear His voice so clearly when I go through difficult times, but when everything is good, I feel distant from God. I struggled at first, comparing my walk with God to other Christians who just seemed "there." I was striving to get where they were, not understanding why I couldn't. My problem was that I was more intellectually saved rather than radically saved. I sought knowledge over Jesus, with the motivation being that I wanted to sound like I knew what I was talking about with all of my Christian friends (just still trying to find worth, right?). It is interesting… Some people are intellectually saved. The evidence is clear to them that Jesus lived on earth, died, and rose again and that God created the world. They collect knowledge to confirm this instead of searching for God himself. That is enough to be intellectually saved. For some, I think people seek salvation in works. They think, "if I keep all of the commands and don't sin, I am safe." Searching for religion and rules instead of abiding in God himself. I want to be radically saved, which is understanding that we were created to be loved and pour out that love on others. That is what I want, and that is what I wish for you.

I was envious of the radically saved Christians. I became utterly frustrated that I was not "there," but all I was missing was just spending time with the Lord and letting Him tell me how much He loved me. Like any relationship, it takes time to build one with God. It takes a lot of getting into the word, being in a community where you can talk about God safely, comparing his character to your experiences, and honestly just sitting in silence with Him. The more you invest, the more the Holy Spirit will work in your relationship with God. Don't get weary in your relationship, don't be afraid that you might find something that will test your faith. Keep seeking. Keep praying about your walk with Him. I truly believe that God will reveal Himself to you over this time if you ask Him. Keep your heart open to Him, and focus on Him. Luckily for us, the same spirit that raised Jesus from the dead lives within us and is interceding for us.

> *Romans 8: 26-27 "In the same way, the Spirit helps us in our weakness. We do not know what we ought to pray for, but the Spirit himself intercedes for us through wordless groans. And he who searches our hearts knows the mind of the Spirit, because the Spirit intercedes for God's people in accordance with the will of God."*

I know we talked a little bit about the consumption of social media adding to our comparison earlier, but that isn't the root problem. It is a mind-numbing distraction keeping us from addressing it. Do you ever find yourself agitated while scrolling? That you need more and more, and it's not necessarily filling you up? The dopamine released from scrolling doesn't equate to fulfillment. But how do we stop these patterns, so we don't waste our precious time in this world?

If comparison is the issue, gratitude is an excellent remedy. Gratitude can be difficult, though. Everyone frames it as easy, you know? Like, be thankful you aren't sleeping outside. Of course, I'm grateful for that, but it's hard to understand unless you've had to live outside. An excellent place to start with gratitude is looking back on your life. I've walked through a lot of dark valleys. By looking back and realizing where I am today is so incredible. I'm so grateful to be out of a lot of things. Something good to put into your daily routine is noting three things you are thankful for each morning.

There is this man A.J. Jacobs who immerses himself in different lifestyles as an experiment for a certain period of time. For one of his experiments, he had to live by all Old Testament commands for a year. This man took it to the extreme too. He even threw rocks at an adulterer, haha, but he got a few life-altering habits out of this experiment. The most significant takeaway from his experient was that praying a prayer of thanksgiving every day, even though he is agnostic, helped him change his perspective on life. So, instead of focusing on what you don't have or the discrepancy between where you are and where you want to be, try practicing gratitude for today and where you are now. You will begin to see the blessings that constantly surround you once you focus on them.

In addition to practicing daily gratitude, let's talk about another daily practice that can change your life: self-love at the mirror. You can look in your eyes in the mirror every day, say positive affirmations to yourself, and grow in self-acceptance. Many studies have been done to back this practice. I want you to try it using scripture. Look into your eyes in front of the mirror and tell yourself one of the below truths. Try it. It is so awkward, but it pays off long-term.

This is what God says about you:

> You are justified and redeemed. (Romans 3:24).

> Your old self was crucified with Christ, and you are no longer a slave to sin. (Romans 6:6).

> You will not be condemned by God. (Romans 8:1).

> You are a child of God and a fellow heir with Christ. (Romans 8:17).

> In Christ Jesus, you have wisdom, righteousness, sanctification, and redemption. (1 Corinthians 1:30).

> Your body is a temple of the Holy Spirit who dwells in Jesus. (1 Corinthians 6:19)

> You are chosen, holy, and blameless before God. (Ephesians 1:4).

> You are redeemed and forgiven by the grace of Christ. (Ephesians 1:7).

> You have been sealed with the Holy Spirit of promise. (Ephesians 1:13).

> You were formerly darkness but now are light in the Lord. (Ephesians 5:8).

> The peace of God guards your heart and mind. (Philippians 4:7).

> God supplies all of your needs. (Philippians 4:19).

> God loves you and has chosen you. (1 Thessalonians 1:4).

> God knit you together in your mother's womb (Psalm 139:13).

> Everything about you is beautiful, and there is nothing at all wrong with you (Song of Solomon 4:7)

Speak that over yourself in the morning. Look dead into your own eyes and say, "I am fearfully and wonderfully made. Through Christ, I have wisdom, righteousness, and I am redeemed. My body is a temple beautifully created to house the powerful Spirit of God. I am chosen and loved." That is who God says that you are through Jesus. Are you going to let the world, with its ever-changing standards, entice you and change you, or are you going to rest in the fact that God has already told you who you are? You are loved, you were created with purpose, you are molded by the hands of the most incredible artist that has ever been! You are a work of art. I hope and pray that God will reveal that to you during this time.

Questions:

1. In what ways are you tempted to change yourself?

    _____

    _____

    _____

    _____

    _____

2. Do these align with the truths that God has already spoken over you?

    _____

    _____

    _____

    _____

    _____

3. Is there anything God told you specifically while reading this?

    _____

    _____

    _____

    _____

    _____

PRAYER: Father, our story is personal and looks like no one around us, which can be difficult sometimes, but also a blessing. We want to learn why you made us the way you did and embrace the purpose behind it. We want to use our lives to set others free. Help us focus not on what we don't have but on the opportunities you are placing in front of us every day. We are so grateful for this beautiful earth you have set us on. Thank you that you created it so that we could enjoy it and constantly be reminded of your splendor.

DAY 17

─w▪◦◖❁◗◦▪w─

LONELINESS

♪

Song: Never Leave - Maverick City
Music, Naomi Raine, Alton Eugene

I have this incredible friend who once told me, "One thing all single people share is some feeling of loneliness, which we resist and try to suppress, refusing to admit that we have this desire and end up hiding this perceived weakness from ourselves and others. However, I don't think that loneliness is a weakness. I think it is God pressing on our hearts, giving us a physical feeling to call us to seek Him and His love, as well as to find a companion on earth to serve and grow with. So, I think instead of trying to resist that loneliness or hide from yourself, you should lean into it and explore that feeling. Why do you feel that way? Are you actually alone? And then, take that emotional nudge that God is giving you to seek Him and His knowledge and learn more about yourself, God, and others. If you do that, you'll feel the loneliness subside, not when or because you've found someone, but because you'll understand that you're enough, valued, loved, and never alone due to what Jesus has already done for you. Embrace this challenge that God has given you, and use this opportunity to grow."

Loneliness is a physical sensation. It makes itself known; it's a feeling that you can't ignore, one that taunts us and causes us to seek a solution. Scientifically, prolonged loneliness can harm your body. Some scientists even compare it to smoking 15 cigarettes a day, which feels a bit dramatic. God created us to be in community. He said in the very beginning, "It is not good for man to be alone (Gen. 2:18)." (Sidebar: once again, science backing the way God told us to live is good for us). While loneliness is not good, I think my friend is right. God uses it to pull us *closer*. He is pressing on our hearts and inviting us to spend some time with Him so that He can tell you how much He loves you.

When I was going through my breakup, the loneliness hit fast and hard. The trigger could be anything from a commercial to a picture on Instagram, but once triggered, I felt it deep. If I could compare the feeling to any earthly thing, maybe I would compare it to quicksand, engulfing my heart and mind little by little. Each time I tried to pull away, it would suck me in more. Knowing that God was there during that time was comforting because I knew I wasn't completely alone. Still, my misunderstanding of God kept me sinking deeper and deeper into that feeling. If only I had known that God could heal my pain and that He wanted to use that time to talk to me. If only I had known, I could trust Him, that He was good, and that He loved me. If only I had known that I didn't have to earn His love. If only I knew the real gospel.

Previously I mentioned the verse Genesis 2:18, *"it is not good for man to be alone."* It comes from the story of God creating Adam and Eve. I recently read the book *Eve* by W.M. Paul that beautifully depicted loneliness. Paul used his poetic imagination to tell a fictional version of the Adam and Eve story that rationalized Adam's choice to sin by showing how the enemy made Adam think he was alone. The following excerpt depicts God and Adam discussing his feeling of loneliness.

"God gently reached around His son, embracing him. "Love takes risks, dear one. You have the freedom to say no to Us, no to Love, to turn your face away." Adam frowned. "And if I did such a thing, what would happen?"

"In turning, you would find yourself within a shadow. This darkening would become more real to you than I am. From then, until you re turned your face to Mine, this empty nothingness would deceive you about everything, including who We [the Trinity] are to you, and who you are to all creation."

I love that passage from the book. God is the light of the world. If you are looking toward the light, you will see no darkness at all. If you turn away from the light, you would see a shadow of yourself. Your shadow self is made up of darkness that comes from you blocking the light. What's even more is if you are face to face with God, it would never occur to you that you are alone, but when you turn away and face your shadow self, you believe that you are alone. W.M. Paul refers to this as shadow sickness. I think that shadow sickness can be synonymous with or work in tandem with sin, as sin seems to come from a lack of love and light. But he is right. The darkness and loneliness does sometimes seem more real than God. It lies to you about who God is and who you are. It tells you God is nothing, and you are nothing. It is so easy to turn our face from Him, close our eyes, and feel the loneliness. But as my friend from earlier said, it is also an invitation to turn back to God. He says, "*I will never leave you or forsake you* (Hebrews 13:5)." So while we have the choice to say no, we also have the choice to say yes, accept His invitation, and be encompassed by his love.

God even calls himself Ehyeh or "I Am." In the Hebrew language, it is an unconjugated conjugation that really means, "I am that I am," or a better interpretation would be, "Here I am."

One of his names is Here I am. He is right there with you. He's sitting in your room with you, in your car, and in your presence. He is enthralled by you and excited to be in your presence (BEMA Podcast Episode 12).

Diving Deeper:

1. When you feel lonely, make time to practice paying attention to God's presence.
    Take a moment and pray for someone else you think might be experiencing feelings of loneliness. This also might be a great time to reach out to that person!

    _____

    _____

    _____

    _____

    _____

2. Read Psalm 25 and practice lamenting loneliness like David.

    _____

    _____

    _____

    _____

    _____

3. Is there anything God told you specifically while reading this?

    _____

    _____

_____

_____

_____

PRAYER: You have told us that we are never alone. We don't want to turn our face from yours, but sometimes we do. We want to look directly at you, into the light and know that we are surrounded by love in every second. Help us choose into your love when we rely on our own strength and comfort us when we fail to choose in. Each day we learn more about you. We grow in love for you as you do for us. We are so grateful to be surrounded by your glorious love.

DAY 18

GIFT

♪

Song: Most Beautiful / So in Love -
Maverick City Music, Chandler Moore

This is impossibly annoying to hear at first, but this time of singleness is a gift. When you can lift your eyes off of your current circumstances and focus on the other opportunities around you, you might just see that this time could be the best time of your life. I want to save you some time so you can get out and start living.

Start with your friendships. There is no better time than now to lean into your friendships. If you don't already have incredible friends that you love immensely and inspire you, this is the time to find them. You want friends who make you laugh, who encourage you, who challenge you and call you higher, who dance with you (even when you dance like one of those wild balloons outside of a car dealership), who like to do fun things, who love you no matter what, who genuinely care about you, pray for you, and know you. These people will be instrumental in ensuring you know **that you are loved and accepted as is** and have the best time in this sweet season.

When I say loved and accepted as is, I genuinely mean that. Every person has that 2% that we hide from our friends due to shame or guilt. It is due to this deep-seeded fear we all have of being unlovable. We ALL have this fear, and more than likely, whatever that piece of you is that you deem "unlovable," there are way more people who are experiencing/have experienced it than you think. Trust me when I say this; it is critical to have at least one person you tell everything to. Whether that be a therapist, friend, or a stranger in a nursing home, it is instrumental that you know that no matter what you have done or what has happened in your life, **you are loved**. The enemy has this way of convincing us that if someone knew what happened to us or if they really knew the dark things we've done or currently struggle with, they will abandon us, judge us, and hurt us. That is a BOLD FACE LIE. You are loved by a God that knows all of your darkest secrets, and He wants you to have friends that will show you that humans, just like God, can accept you and love you despite your past or your current circumstances. Being fully seen and fully loved is big-time prep for your next relationship. If you know that your friends love you, you can be confident that a man will love you as is, dark and twisties and all. Now, I am not saying you have to tell everyone all of your deepest secrets, but when you trust someone and feel led to open up to them, don't let the fear of judgment or shame stop you. The enemy will make it seem like your life as you know it will be over if you tell someone, but really you will begin to live in freedom. And in your freedom, you will set others free.

Read Psalm 91:9-16 as a reminder of God's protection over us.

Let's get back to talking about the gift that this season is. Get to know yourself. Do you know who you really are? And not the 3-minute elevator pitch that is a combination of what people have told you you are good at or excel in and what you do. No, your real identity, who God says you are. I bet people have thrown false identities on you your whole life. I remember a moment in middle school when a new girl came to my school who knew one of my dance friends, and she said, "Wow, you aren't fat. __ said you were bigger." From that day on, "fat" was tied to my identity. I think almost every girl I know has identified with that at some point. People, especially those who don't know their own identity, will throw all kinds of false labels on you. And you subconsciously adopt them as well.

It is essential to pay attention to the "I am" statements that come out of your mouth or even live in your head—every time you say. "I am __," your subconscious is paying attention. Your words hold a lot of power. They have the ability to build up or slowly destroy. Next time you find yourself saying that you "are" something, cross-reference it with the truth. Here are some common ones to address, I am worthless, ugly, annoying, fake, too much, too quiet, ignorant, dumb, emotional, mean, lazy, unmotivated, selfish, loose, out of control, unlovable, and the list goes on. If you have ever been falsely labeled, it is essential to abandon those lies immediately and replace them with the truth. The truth of your identity is that you are beloved, beautiful, daughter, heir, friend, worthy, righteous, **good**, delightful, funny, fun to be around, and made in the image of God. If you identify with anything contrary, it's time to confront those identities and repent from that way of thinking. Repent just means that every time the enemy enters your mind to tell you something like, "you are disgusting," you actively say no and choose to believe that you are beautiful. Remember, observing and redirecting your thoughts will form new neural pathways, and each time you do it, your brain will become more likely to default to true and positive thoughts. Spiritual speaker Jamie Winship says this, "insecurities flare when we aren't secure in our identity in Christ." So fight to believe who your Father in heaven tells you you are.

We are always trying to change parts about ourselves that God created with a purpose. I used to hate that I was introverted, over-analytical, cried all of the time, and laughed too loud or too hard. I hated my singing voice, loud inner critic, body, and "talents" that seemed pretty useless. But it is hilarious how when you lean closer to God, he reveals that each part of us that we "hate" was designed intentionally and is part of His plan for our life. He is a redeemer. To give you an example, I have always been insecure about being an introvert. Our society values extroverts immensely, and truthfully, my self-esteem caught on to that way before I learned about it in the business world. I always tried to push myself to say more quantity over quality. "Just say something," I would tell myself in social settings with new people, but I never could force myself to be that way. But, God has shown me that there is massive value in being introverted: the ability to listen, to observe, to empathize, and to be comfortable alone are just a few. I am not saying that extroverts aren't great at these things, either. God has shown me personally why He created me this way, as I am sure that He will show you too if you let Him.

Also, as uncomfortable as this may sound, you should give "dating" yourself a try. This act is super foreign at first and a little cringy, but you will crave this time once you try it. In one of my last bible studies, I met a girl who told me she took herself on dinner dates every month. To me, this sounded excruciatingly awkward and lonely, but part of me was intrigued. I like to conduct social experiments in my own life, and this new experience sounded like a great one, so I went. I set aside some money and went to a nice dinner by myself. It was indeed awkward at first. I weirdly put shame on myself for being in public alone. I thought people would think I was sad, but in reality, no one was paying much attention to me at all. After the initial awkwardness, it was enjoyable. I brought a good book, ate an INCREDIBLE meal, and had a nice glass of wine. It was so much fun, and when I got back, I had the apartment to myself. I turned on some music and just sang and danced around the room like some kind of wild alien girl. I had too much fun, and what resulted was a lessening of my fear of man and a newfound appreciation of time spent alone enjoying good food with the Father. I encourage you to try it.

Next, try getting into the habit of setting goals if you are not accustomed to it. I have never been one to set goals or try to achieve anything out of the ordinary. I thought that that was part of my makeup. But I discovered that most people who do not form a vision or goals for their lives live in protection mode, not creation mode. One of many reasons this could happen is because you were not provided proper safety as a child. Safety from verbal abuse, yelling, physical abuse, divorce, neglect, stressful environments, etc. And if you were put in stressful/harmful situations enough, you probably began looking out for yourself and trying to predict outcomes of situations to protect yourself. You were taught, by nature, to live in a permanent state of alert. If you are always looking around to shield yourself, you will never look forward and create future goals. But, God wants us to co-create our lives with Him. He wants our opinions and buy-in on what our future looks like. He wants us to set goals and invite Him in while listening out for his still small voice in all of it. So set some goals! Once you start, it's addicting.

During quarantine, my best friend and I set a goal to run a half marathon and read through the whole New Testament. If you know anything about me, I am long and a little clumsy. I never thought my body could handle running 4 miles, much less 13. I started microscopic, half a mile, and then ran a little more each day. Eventually, we were able to run a half marathon. I never felt so optimistic about my body's capabilities. I was the only thing holding myself back. We also read through the whole New Testament (well, I listened to it on the Youversion app). Doing both together and having a friend to keep me accountable showed me that I was much stronger mentally and physically than I thought, and I know you are too.

Lastly, this whole study is obviously about getting to know God during this time. Create space to get to know Him more intimately. Carve out dinners, mornings, nights, whatever time you can to spend time with Him. He is worth it. My whole heart just exploded, thinking about the goodness that has come through spending time with Him. It has removed my own false identity, taken off the false identity I put on God, broken me, and made me whole again. Start with a simple way to incorporate God into your day that you enjoy, and be patient and expectant for the newness and deeper levels that will follow. Also, God is so funny. No one ever told me that. He literally created humor so just expect to learn that side of Him. It is such a sweet time to get to know Him and the many facets of His incredibly loving and kind heart.

What if tomorrow you meet the man that you are going to marry? Did you get to do all of the things you wanted to do during your time of singleness? Did you grow in all of the ways you needed to before attempting to become one flesh with someone else? Once you meet the one, your time will be divided, and you will be missing time with friends and the alone time you have now! Embrace this beautiful time. It is a gift.

Diving Deeper:

1. To open up that 2% that you might be hiding choose a person you are thinking about opening up to, and pray for God to give you the strength to do so. Pray for an ear to hear when and who to open up to. If this feels like too much, maybe consider finding a counselor and pray about that as well.

   _____

   _____

   _____

   _____

   _____

2. How do you want to get to know yourself further during this time?

   _____

   _____

   _____

_____

_____

3. If you feel genuine about wanting to seek God, tell Him that. Ask Him to reveal Himself to you at deeper levels during this time.

_____

_____

_____

_____

_____

4. Is there anything God told you specifically while reading this?

_____

_____

_____

_____

_____

PRAYER: Thank you for this time. Even though it gets hard sometimes, we want to see it for the gift that it is. We want more of you. You are our treasure and our greatest reward. We stand in awe of your glory. Your gaze, your attention, and your affection are all-consuming. Direct our path during this time and help us focus on our opportunities and not what we are missing. Who can we serve? Who can we encourage? Who can we lift up? What do you want to develop within us? You have given us this supernatural strength and tenacity that we want to give to those around us who are in need of it. We bless your name. You are so good.

DAY 19

———∿∿∽◦⦿◦⦾◦⦿◦∿∿———

MATCHMAKER

♪

Song: Real Thing - Maverick
City Music, Dante Bowe

What if you did meet your soulmate tomorrow? I love to discuss the age-old debate of whether or not there is a single person, or "soulmate," for each of us. Whether or not you believe in soulmates, it is important to know that God is a matchmaker, and He is a really good one. As a matchmaker, He has an incredible man or, based on your beliefs, multiple men in mind for you. One who exemplifies His perfect love. One who will make you further understand God's love for you and bring you closer to Him. How do you know who it is?! My thoughts are that the man that God has for you will pursue your heart in the same way that Jesus pursues our hearts.

Let's talk about your future husband a little more. He should probably possess similar qualities to Jesus. I want you to dig into the nature of Jesus in this next section:

Jesus was a servant. He said it all the time. He came to serve, not to be served (Matthew 20:28). Service is truly synonymous with love, and it goes both ways. When you find a man who is willing to serve you, serve others, and, more importantly, one who you are eager to serve, that's a good sign that you are on the right path. Check. Next.

Jesus loved verbally. Find a man who affirms every part of you and not just for your STUNNING good looks but also for the characteristics that reflect who you truly are and who God made you to be. He needs to be able to remind you of your God-given identity when you can't see it. Check. Next.

Jesus loved respectfully. If you ever feel that your opinions or boundaries are not being respected by a suitor.... BY A SUITOR?!... That is not okay. He is supposed to be pursuing you in the dating phase of the relationship, not inflating his ego by putting you down or making you feel like you aren't of any value without what your body brings to the table. You need someone who respects your thoughts, opinions, and boundaries and encourages you to grow, just like Jesus would have. Check. Next.

Jesus loved faithfully. When someone is not faithful to you, it shoots one of those aforementioned arrows at your heart, telling you that you are not worthy, making you want that person's acceptance all the more. It is a mind game that the enemy loves for us to play. So, as hard as it is to break things off when your significant other is not faithful, it is important. You deserve a man who chooses you as his life partner over and over again, just like God has chosen humanity over and over again. Check. Next.

Jesus loved extravagantly. This extravagant love was displayed best by the sacrifice of Jesus' life. One great example is when He turned water into wine. And not just a small amount, it ended up being 600-900 bottles of wine in addition to the wine that was already served at the feast. That is extravagant. The man pursuing you should love extravagantly and pull out all the stops. He doesn't have to shower you with gifts to do this either. Extravagance can be displayed through time, energy, and intentionality as well. He should be able to do this with what he has. Check. Next.

Jesus pursued us. As I mentioned earlier in the section that discussed Hosea, God has pursued humanity throughout our time on earth. He has pursued us when we've drawn near and when we've pushed Him away. You shouldn't feel as if you have to be someone else or compromise your values in order to be pursued. Your future husband should be asking you to hang out with Him, making his intentions very clear, getting to know you, and wanting to spend ample time with you. Check. Next.

Most importantly, Jesus revealed the heart of the Father. Revealing God's true nature and character was the center of Jesus' whole ministry. He said, "Anyone who has seen me has seen the Father (John 14:9)." If you are ever wondering how God would react to an action, just look at how Jesus reacted. He showed us that God was wildly misunderstood, and He is good and loves abundantly. In your dating relationship, you should further come to understand who the Father is because the man you are dating shows you love in a way you have never been shown before.

I will stop there, but I urge you to look into more ways that Jesus loved us. There are SO MANY. Look, I get that these are high-ish standards, but I never want you to think, "beggars can't be choosers." First of all, beggars were INVALUABLE to Jesus, and in His kingdom, beggars can be choosers. Secondly, if you doubt that a man like this exists, I know so many single, INCREDIBLE, attractive, fun men of God who are very much like this. You probably aren't running across them because of your current social circle. If you want to meet a man who reflects the Lord, you'll probably need to find some social circles filled with people that reflect the Lord. They are probably currently serving others, reading the Word, and waiting on someone like you to turn to God and jump in headfirst. Let me say that again, turn to God, not turn to a man.

I want to challenge you to start by making good Christian guy friends. They will hopefully show you how a good Christian man should treat you. You need to get used to being respected, talking about Jesus in your relationships, and trying to mend the relationship with men that might have been twisted at some point or another. If you don't currently have any, go to a church and join a coed small group.

When will you find him? People often say, "When you stop looking for a man, he will show up." There is some truth to that statement. It is always tricky, though, because if your heart is not fully healed, you will end up being disingenuous about not trying to actively find someone, and you will be looking for a significant other while claiming you aren't. As I said, I did that. I say this so that you can take some of the pressure off. If you try to look at every man as a friend first, they will let you know if they want to pursue something more. If not, great, you are a woman of God who just made a new friend who will show you the characteristics you want in a husband.

But remember our story about Abraham from the section on prayer. God is not going to tell you when or how you will meet your husband, probably because we all would mess it up if He did. God might be hiding you away for a season. He might want you all to Himself for a little while. He craves the alone time that He gets with you and because He wants more, you are hidden. That's a good thing, friends. Honestly, that's an honor and a prize. While He has you, He wants you to learn to love Him and to love yourself before jumping into that sacred relationship that He has for you.

Trust that God knows you. He "*knit you together* (Psalm 139:13)." He chose every part of your personality. He has a man in mind for you who will love you in a way that will bring glory to God and bring others to Christ. He will be the person you spend the most time with and the person you listen to the most, so he MUST be speaking life into you and pointing you back to Jesus in every moment. The world can be a hard place to live and navigate. You need your other half to push you towards the light, not pull you into darkness. Your Father loves you so much, and He believes with His whole heart that you were created beautifully and with a purpose. You are worth loving, and you are worth loving abundantly.

Diving Deeper:

1. Investigate the life of Jesus. Maybe flip to any chapter in Matthew, Mark, Luke, or John and read a section about Him. How else did He love us?

   _____

   _____

   _____

   _____

   _____

2. Is there anything God told you specifically while reading this?

_____

_____

_____

_____

_____

PRAYER: Father, dating is difficult. The path to this point has been paved with heartbreak. We know that was never your or even our intention. We want the relationship you have for us that brings goodness and life to everyone around us. We do not want to settle for anything less than a person who reflects you. Open our eyes to truly see men who love you and give us an aversion to romantic relationships with men who still need to take from us. We want to see the reflection of your love on Earth in our next dating relationship.

DAY 20

FILLED WITH THE SPIRIT

♪

Song: Rest On Us - Maverick
City Music x Upperroom

Something that I never could fully grasp in my relationship with God, previous to my breakup, was the Holy Spirit. If you are diving into the word for the first time, I can only imagine how foreign this concept sounds. The Holy Spirit is a part of the trinity: God, Jesus, and the Spirit. Three in one. They exemplify love because love is relational. While I could go on, I encourage you to look into it; The Bible Project is a great place to start. What does this have to do with singleness, you ask? Well, I believe that in singleness, your impact on the world has the potential to be huge. I say potential because learning how to submit to the Holy Spirit determines how huge your impact could be.

The Spirit first comes on the scene in the first page of the Bible. Genesis 1:2-3 *"Now the earth was formless and empty, darkness was over the surface of the deep, and the **Spirit of God** was hovering over* *the waters." And God said, "Let there be light," and there was light."* So, if you are reading the Bible without really digging into the Hebrew translation here, you could miss this. Tim Macke broke this down BEAUTIFULLY in his series on the Holy Spirit in his podcast Exploring my Strange Bible. In our Bibles, we see the words "Spirit of God" and that the Spirit was hovering over the waters, but in Hebrew, it is a little more involved than just "Spirit." The Hebrew word is Ruach meaning "breath, spirit." Do something quickly for me. Hold up your hand to your mouth and start speaking. Do you feel that coming out? That is your breath, right? When God spoke the words "Let there be light," He breathed them out using His Ruach, which means that He used his Spirit in the creation of the world. The Spirit is a tool to create and change.

So, how is the Spirit relevant to us? First, let's talk about Pentecost. Read **Acts 2.** It is a little long, but it is **very** important that you read it.

I wanted us to read that passage to show the power of the Spirit and that since Christ died for us, the Spirit was poured out and now dwells within us. When we seek Jesus with all of our heart, we are given the Spirit, and that Spirit is the same Spirit that raised Christ from the dead. THAT'S INSANE. That's powerful. The Spirit doesn't always come on us with miraculous signs. It isn't some religious magic trick that we can use to perform with, but the Spirit is powerful. The Spirit creates and changes, new life is formed within us, and we begin to shift naturally. With the Spirit, you are empowered and directed.

What do we do with this Spirit, and how will it change us? I am going to use Tim Macke's analogy about gardening. I love gardening. If you have never grown a plant before in your life, you need to try it ASAP. You feel so accomplished when you plant a seed, watch it sprout, and see it continue to grow. How does the plant grow, though? Are we, as humans pulling it up out of the ground? No, plants grow on their own. We don't do anything but tend to the plant: watering it, trimming it, making sure it has enough sunlight. It is the same thing with the Spirit. When we accept Christ, we receive the Spirit, but we have to tend to the Spirit for change to happen. Don't get me wrong, once we accept Jesus, we are stamped and are given the Spirit for life. But we can either tend to the Spirit by focusing on our relationship with the Father: reading scripture, spending quiet time with God, and being in fellowship with other believers. Or, we can just live our lives with the Spirit, not sprouting or growing any fruit.

We are given a clear-cut picture of what should happen when we tend to the Spirit. We display the FRUIT OF THE SPIRIT. Not fruits of the Spirit. It's one fruit. Check it out:

Galatians 5:22-23 "But the fruit of the Spirit is love, joy, peace, forbearance, kindness, goodness, faithfulness, gentleness and self-control."

If we are tending to the Spirit, giving it light and water, it will bear fruit in our lives. When I was younger, this was framed incorrectly to me. It was explained like this: "The fruits of the Spirit are guidelines to how you should be acting as a Christian. If you are lacking in one fruit, you should work on that." That feels like faith by works to me. Instead, it should be that if we are focused on our relationship with our Father, getting to know the real Him and his true love for us, the Spirit will grow within us, and we will see the fruit of that growth. As in, the Spirit will change you and make you loving, joyful, peaceful. It will give you self-control. It will make you kind, good, faithful, and gentle. You don't need to focus on your self-control if you are lacking there. No, you need to focus on Jesus and walk toward Him, and this fruit will come with that growth. Cool, right?! So, this isn't about changing your rules for life or trying harder to live right. Just lean into Jesus and tend to the Spirit.

Additionally, the Bible talks about gifts of the Spirit:

> *1 Corinthians 12: 7-11 "The Holy Spirit is given to each of us in a special way. That is for the good of all. To some people the Spirit gives a message of wisdom. To others the same Spirit gives a message of knowledge. To others the same Spirit gives faith. To others that one Spirit gives gifts of healing. To others he gives the power to do miracles. To others he gives the ability to prophesy. To others he gives the ability to tell the spirits apart. To others he gives the ability to speak in different kinds of languages they had not known before. And to still others he gives the ability to explain what was said in those languages. All the gifts are produced by one and the same Spirit. He gives gifts to each person, just as he decides."*

There are probably hundreds of more gifts like discernment, burden-bearing, teaching, the gift of faith, etc. Some Christians believe that the Spirit doesn't give gifts like this anymore and that they died with the publishing of the Bible. That is what I was told, but it doesn't say anywhere in the Bible that God stopped the Spirit from giving us gifts because we don't need them anymore. I think we need them now more than ever. I was told that speaking in tongues was demonic. How did we, as Christians, get to a place where a gift of the Spirit was thought of as demonic?. I personally believe that the gifts are active because the Spirit is active. And that they are incredible tools to help build the kingdom. I do caution that pursuing gifts over pursuing God is where many people miss the boat and end up misusing them for power, control, or influence. That is not the intention with these gifts. They are intended to bring the kingdom, give life to those who need it, encourage people, build them up, and help restore people to who the Father created them to be. I have seen the Holy Spirit gift people with these gifts around me, and He has even gifted me with them at times. My encouragement is to understand that you are always in a two-way conversation with God. And He will equip you with the necessary tools at the right time to further His kingdom and to build up / edify Christ's body.

Once again, I believe that your ministry, while single, has the potential to be HUGE. God is working through you constantly. You might not realize that you are using some of these gifts, but they will flow out of you if you are receptive to what God is doing. For example, if you have the gift of discernment, you might be able to tell whether or not people are lying to you. If you have the gift of wisdom, you might give excellent advice and find that people turn to you a lot to receive it. If you have the gift of prophecy, you might know someone's struggles before they tell you and be able to encourage them where they are. Those are just examples, but you can always look into it further. You might not feel qualified or equipped to go out and make a change, but if you stay close to God, you will see his power work through you. You probably already have.

Discussion Questions:

1. Read through the fruit of the spirit and list some ways you have seen your fruit grow.

_____

_____

_____

_____

_____

2. Read through the gifts of the spirit in the passage above (1 Corinthians 12). Are there any that you think you have seen God use through you?

_____

_____

_____

_____

_____

3. Is there anything God told you specifically while reading this?

_____

_____

_____

_____

_____

PRAYER: In learning more about you, we have come to see that you are so much more. Spirit come and rest on us. We want to be filled with you. We want people to stop us and say, "What is different about you? What is coming off of you?" because your Spirit is pouring out of us. Thank you that you came and died so that we could be filled by your spirit. Thank you that you have called us temples of the Holy Spirit. We are so incredibly thankful.

DAY 21

CONTINUING THE FIGHT

♪

Revival's In The Air- Bethel Music

We have previously touched on some defense mechanisms for pain and types of attacks against your relationship with God. Truthfully, the enemy will try everything to get you from taking steps forward with God. He will pull out all of his tricks, and you need to be ready. Today's devotional will help you craft a plan to continue to pursue the Lord.

Let's start with some scripture, and then we will get into the actual tactics:

> *Ephesians 6: 11-18 "Put on the full armor of God, so that you can take your stand against the devil's schemes. For our struggle is not against flesh and blood, but against the rulers, against the authorities, against the powers of this dark world and against the spiritual*

forces of evil in the heavenly realms. Therefore put on the full armor of God, so that when the day of evil comes, you may be able to stand your ground, and after you have done everything, to stand. Stand firm then, with the belt of truth buckled around your waist, with the breastplate of righteousness in place, and with your feet fitted with the readiness that comes from the gospel of peace. In addition to all this, take up the shield of faith, with which you can extinguish all the flaming arrows of the evil one. Take the helmet of salvation and the sword of the Spirit, which is the word of God. And pray in the Spirit on all occasions with all kinds of prayers and requests. With this in mind, be alert and always keep on praying for all the Lord's people."

I love the metaphor of a battle for faith. We are in a battle. It may not be a physical battle but a battle of the mind. Here are some tools to help you move forward in the right direction. For our fight, we need truth, right relationship with God, peace that comes from intimately knowing that we are not slaves to sin anymore but beloved daughters, faith to extinguish the flaming arrows of worthlessness, prayer in the spirit, and alertness.

I want to preface this by saying once more, faith by works is dead. You were created to be loved, and God loves you, so check. You are done. Below are the tools that I used and found helpful when fighting in my battle with the enemy.

SCRIPTURE: At the beginning of this journey, I would google verses about pain, redemption, God's love, etc., as a starting point and then read around the verses for context. I bought some sticky notes and covered my mirror with scripture that spoke to me. It was so helpful. If you haven't read the gospels, I would start there. Just observe the way Jesus reacts. If you want to start with the Old Testament, I would highly recommend listening to a podcast such as the BEMA podcast to walk you through it. If you start with episode 1, you will learn some literary tools, types of literature, context, and hidden treasures in the scriptures that you would only know if you were an ancient Jewish scholar. IMPORTANT: Often, if something strikes you as offensive or incongruent with the rest of the text, it is most likely a translation error or a Historical reference that you don't have context for. Google it. Get context.

WORSHIP MUSIC: During an initial season of a breakup or during a time when you feel like you are struggling, surround yourself with worship music. Listen even when you are not sad. Listen while you work, in your car, or falling asleep. Whenever you can. It builds this "holy fortress" around you and keeps your focus on the one who will heal you. The goodness (worship music) that goes into your body will produce goodness to come out. You might hate the worship music you grew up with, but trust me, new and beautiful songs exist. I included my favorites in the sections of this study with my favorites because they have impacted me. God gifted these singers and songwriters with abilities to make you fall on your knees and be overwhelmed by God's love.. You just have to find the ones that speak to you. Bands I recommend: Hillsong United, Maverick City Music, Upperroom, Housefires, Lauren Daigle, etc.

CHRISTIAN MEDIATION: Similar to worship music, Christian meditation can provide a spiritual barrier when loneliness comes. If you feel pain welling up to the point that all other senses are being compromised, stop what you are doing and meditate. During my breakup, I downloaded the Abide app, which has Christian meditations and did that very thing. Every time during the workday, when I would feel the initial onset of pain, I would stop, go into a room, and listen to a meditation. I cried a few tears, sat there for another couple of minutes, and then went back to work. If you do not want to pay for an app, Youtube has some great Christ-centered meditations for free. Scripture even tells us to meditate, which is so cool because studies on meditation show how helpful meditation is in personal growth. Our brains need space and connection to God. He designed us this way.

> Psalms 1:2 *"But his delight is in the law of the LORD, and on his law he meditates day and night."*

> Psalms 119:15 *"I meditate on your precepts and consider your ways."*

> Isaiah 26:3 *"You will keep in perfect peace those whose minds are steadfast, because they trust in you."*

> Joshua 1:8 *"Keep this Book of Law always on your lips; meditate on it day and night so that you may be careful to do everything written in it. Then you will be prosperous and successful."*

PRAYER: As I said in the section on prayer, prayer is a great way to start your relationship with God, but if there is anything we can learn from Paul, it is that prayer is a solid defense as well. As it said in the above scripture, *"our struggle is not against flesh and blood, but against the rulers, against the authorities, against the powers of this dark world and against the spiritual forces of evil in the heavenly realms" (Ephesians 6:12).* This is how we fight those battles in the heavenly realms. We pray to our Father, who has power over all. He fights for us. I could go into another whole section on prayer alone, but I am just going to let the Bible speak instead:

> Philippians 4:6 *"Do not be anxious about anything, but in everything by prayer and supplication with thanksgiving let your requests be made known to God.*

Matthew 26:41 "Watch and pray that you may not enter into temptation. The spirit indeed is willing, but the flesh is weak.

1 Thessalonians 5:16-18 "Rejoice always, pray without ceasing, give thanks in all circumstances; for this is the will of God in Christ Jesus for you."

[Side Note: An important part of prayer is learning to hear God's voice. Two books that I recommend for learning to hear the voice of God are **Whisper** by Mark Batterson and **The Art of the Listening Prayer** by Seth Barnes.]

JOURNALING: I have always heard journaling was a game-changer, and I can tell you from experience it is. Think of journaling as a method of processing. The act of writing down thoughts can help you learn a lot about yourself. Especially for my fellow introverts out there! Writing down our thoughts leads us to realize our true feelings. Also, having documentation to look back on to see what prayers God has answered and how you have grown during your time with Him helps reassure you that He is working.

FASTING: I first fasted after my breakup to dive back into my relationship with God. I fasted social media for a month, and honestly, I was shocked to see how much more time I could devote to God without it. Technically, you could fast anything that the absence of reminds you of God. This is just a suggestion, but it taught me a lot about reliance on God and how He can sustain and fill us.

CHRISTIAN BOOKS: I am an Enneagram Type 1, meaning that I am always looking to refine myself, so I have always loved Christian books. For those of you who are not so interested in the idea of reading a book, perhaps try listening to one. The below books

I am going to list out have changed my perspective on God in the best way:

> **Eve** by WM. Paul
> **Spiritual Slavery to Spiritual Sonship** by Jack Frost
> **Unashamed** by Christine Caine
> **Get Lost** by Dannah Gresh
> **Get Out of Your Mind** by Jennie Allen
> **Irresistible** by Andy Stanley
> **Redeeming Love** by Francine Rivers

PODCASTS: When you want to learn about God but aren't in the mood to read, go to the podcasts below.

> **BEMA podcast** - #1 BEST PODCAST to understand scripture. I don't agree with everything they say, but most are GOLD.

> **Exploring My Strange Bible** - SO HELPFUL to further your learning about scripture. love Tim Macke (also look into The Bible Project videos that help explain each book of the Bible)

> **Any podcast with Jamie Winship or Christine Caine** (if you have the podcasts app, search for "Jesus in Your Boat" - Jaime Winship and "156: Jamie Winship: Living an Unconflicted Life") THEY ARE ENTIRELY TOO GOOD.

CHURCH: I touched on this earlier, but in my opinion, the modern church is not what it was ever supposed to be, but it is still a great place to find community. It is also not a one-size-fits-all, so you might have to try multiple churches before you find a good fit. Also, try joining a small group. They are more similar to some of the first churches mentioned in the New Testament than what we have today. So find your own "church." Just make sure it is a place where you are surrounded by a body of believers who uplift and encourage you in the right direction, that you are talking about scripture, and that Christ is at the head of it.

GIVE BACK: Find what breaks your heart and start figuring out ways to help. You might already be involved with a non-profit, but if not, ask around! There are great charities that help feed the hungry, provide shelter to those who need it, rehabilitate wounded people, plant trees, and foster animals. These are great ways to spread the love of Jesus, meet people, and see how the Holy Spirit can change lives through your words of encouragement. My advice is to get to know at least one person on a deeper level each time you volunteer.

WATCH THE CHOSEN: For easy consumption of the New Testament, download The Chosen app to watch a semi-accurate show about the life of Jesus. This is not a replacement for reading scripture, but it is an incredible show. I have cried during every episode.

All of this probably seems overwhelming, but I wanted to equip you with several different tools so that you could choose the ones that sound right for you. If you are paralyzed with where to start, I would start with learning how to read scripture.

Diving Deeper:

1. Write out a plan from this list of how you will continue your journey after this devotional.

    Example:
    Read a chapter of Luke a day
    Listen to 1 Christian book this year

Listen to worship music or a podcast in the shower
or on your drive to work
Meditate once a week

_____

_____

_____

_____

_____

_____

_____

_____

_____

_____

_____

_____

_____

2. Is there anything God told you specifically while reading this?

_____

_____

_____

_____

CLOSING NOTE

As you learn to experience God during this season, don't forget his promises. Your life, your love, and most importantly, you move the heart of the creator of the world. He loves everything you are. He is captivated by you. You absolutely blow Him away.

I want to tell you that I, personally, am having a difficult time not being able to be there to walk you through any questions or emotions. The fixer in me wants to try to control, but I know that God is ready to further this healing, and He can do FAR more than I could ever. I just ask that if this devotional reopened any wounds that you feel need to be addressed further, seek out some professional help.

As we close up, I just want to say thank you for reading! I want to pray over you as you continue on this journey: God, as I prayed when we began this devotional, I pray again for this reader to develop a thirst for you. I pray for healing over their wounds and that you continue to open their eyes to see how much you care about them. I know that you are the great healer and that even though we have reopened some of these wounds, you are there to stitch them together again. You are really good, really sweet, and really fun. Continue to reveal yourself in significant ways. Continue to show your plan for this reader's life as you see fit. It is not small. It will bring others from the brink of depression and suicide. It will restore hope and love to families. It is big. God, I pray for protection from lies over them and endurance to fight the battle. You are able to do more than we could ever dream. WE LOVE YOU SO MUCH.

ACKNOWLEDGMENTS

I'm so grateful for all of the incredible people in my life who have led me to this point. Of course, the path of healing and growth is an infinite journey, but I am excited about where I am today. I want to say thanks to my family and friends. While this was a strange idea, you each encouraged me to write this devotional and told me that I wasn't wasting my time.

I want to thank my brother Tom who was the person who helped me begin my real journey with God. I wouldn't know the incredible love of God I know today without him. Thanks to my friends who supported me during this time: Grace, Ashley, Leigh, Rebecca, Emma, Cassidy, Sam, Whit, Danny, Shelby, Jess, Jessica, Lisa, Marisa, Rachel, Caroline, Clayton, Max, and Chris. My friends who helped me edit and develop this devotional: Kristi Robinson, Rachel Snow, Jessica Pickens, Anna Lofgren, Caroline Sedgwick, and Chris Smith. Caroline and Rachel walked through the whole devotional with me and helped me develop many of these ideas.

I want to thank my therapist, Dr. Forde, for walking me through a lot of healing and teaching me many of these lessons. I want to thank the powerful women in my life: Ros Try-hane, Patrallia Davis-Bryant, and of course, my mom. Also, my incredible G42 leaders: Gary and Lisa Black, Ethan and Kristen Wendle, Zach and Meagan Ripley, Morgan Foldes, Linley and Matt Krahel, Katie and Will Boggs, and Andrew and Mo Shearman. You have taught me more than you will ever know about the Father's heart.

And lastly, to people I don't have a personal relationship with but have destroyed my limited perception of God and taught me more about who He is: Tim Mackie, Jamie Winship, Christine Caine, Marty Sullivan, Brent Billings, and Andy Stanley.

ABOUT THE AUTHOR

If you don't know me, hi, I'm Sarah Pond. I'm a 27-year-old work in progress. To tell you a little bit of my testimony: I experienced a lot of trauma at a young age that spanned a long period of time. My whole family did. While my path looked slightly different from theirs, we all spun out. We searched for worth and identity in peers, partying, relationships, and achievements. Trust me when I say that I've been the prodigal son and the proud older brother. Thank God that He came for the sick. He completely transformed my life. I've been to low lows and high highs. While I kept a lot of this vague, I want you to know that if you've experienced trauma, you aren't alone. God took my struggles and pain and has used them to set others free. He set me free. He has redeemed me and made me new, and so now, my greatest passion is to remove the false identity that has been put on God and tell the world that He actually is so good.

Printed in the United States
by Baker & Taylor Publisher Services